PUB WALK

— IN —

Dartmoor &
South Devon

Other areas covered in the Pub Walks series include:

Bedfordshire
Berkshire
Bristol and Bath
Buckinghamshire
Cambridgeshire
Cheshire
Chilterns
Cotswolds
County Durham
Derbyshire
Essex
Exmoor & North Devon
Gloucestershire
Hampshire & the New Forest
Herefordshire
Hertfordshire
Kent
Leicestershire and Rutland
Lincolnshire

North London
Middlesex & West London
Norfolk
Northamptonshire
Nottinghamshire
Oxfordshire
Shropshire
South Downs
Staffordshire
Suffolk
Surrey
Thames Valley
Warwickshire
Wiltshire
Worcestershire
East Yorkshire
North Yorkshire
South Yorkshire
West Yorkshire

PUB WALKS
IN
Dartmoor &
South Devon

THIRTY CIRCULAR WALKS
AROUND DARTMOOR & SOUTH DEVON INNS

Michael Bennie

COUNTRYSIDE BOOKS
NEWBURY, BERKSHIRE

Designed by Mon Mohan
Cover illustration by Colin Doggett
Photographs by the author
Maps by Jonathan Bennie

Produced through MRM Associates Ltd., Reading
Typeset by Paragon Typesetters, Queensferry, Clwyd
Printed in England

Contents

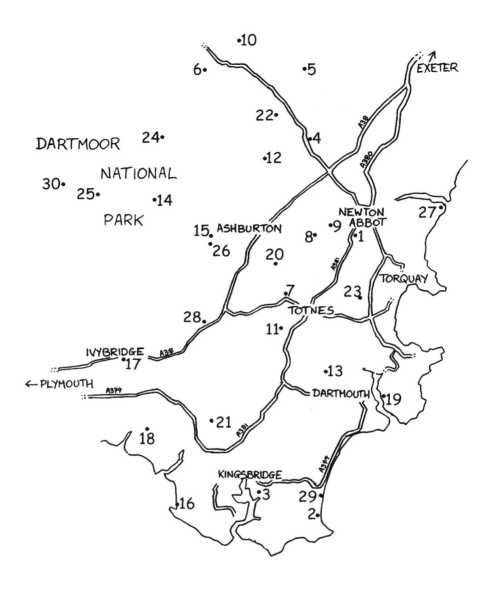

Area map showing locations of the walks.

Publisher's Note

We hope that you obtain considerable enjoyment from this book; great care has been taken in its preparation. However, changes of landlord and actual closures are sadly not uncommon. Likewise, although at the time of publication all routes followed public rights of way or permitted paths, diversion orders can be made and permissions withdrawn.

We cannot, of course, be held responsible for such diversion orders and any inaccuracies in the text which might result from these or any other changes to the routes nor any damage which might result from walkers trespassing on private property. We are anxious though that all details covering the walks are kept up to date and would therefore welcome information from readers which would be relevant to future editions.

The sketch maps accompanying each walk are not always to scale and are intended to guide you to the starting point and give a simple but accurate idea of the route to be taken. For those who like the benefit of detailed maps, we recommend that you arm yourself with the relevant Ordnance Survey map.

Introduction

South Devon has one of the most varied landscapes of any area in Britain, from rugged coastal cliffs to rich rolling farmland, from high, wild moors to idyllic wooded valleys. And despite the fact that it is one of the most popular holiday areas in the country, it is surprisingly easy to get off the beaten track and find hidden corners, unspoilt villages and paths where one can walk for miles without seeing another soul.

In this collection of walks I have tried to reflect the rich variety that is on offer and to provide something for all tastes. Some of the routes visit popular beauty spots; many explore obscure byways that take you far away from the crowds. But wherever you are walking, please remember the Country Code, and do not leave gates open, disturb farm animals, pick wild flowers or leave litter.

A sketch map is provided for each walk to supplement the route description, but if you would like more detail then you can refer to the Ordnance Survey maps indicated. The Explorer maps are more detailed (1:25 000 as opposed to 1:50 000 for the Landranger series), but they cover smaller areas.

The descriptions of the pubs and their surroundings are intended to give an idea of the atmosphere of the place, and are therefore very personal impressions. I have, however, given basic information on all of them.

I am proud of my adopted county, and of its stunningly beautiful scenery and its friendly, welcoming people. I hope that this book will help you to appreciate it too.

Michael Bennie

① Abbotskerswell
The Butcher's Arms

This pretty village nestles in a valley about 1½ miles south-west of Newton Abbot. There are some modern developments, but they are mostly tucked away out of sight behind the old centre of the village, with its pretty traditional cottages and gardens.

The Butcher's Arms is on the edge of the village. Built in 1850, it has in its time been a smithy and a beer house. Now it is a warm, friendly pub which caters for a strong contingent of local regulars as well as visitors. There is just the one bar divided into two areas by a small partition. An interesting collection of blow torches hangs from the beams, and you will also discover farm equipment, lanterns and even a few gas masks. A large fire provides warmth in winter.

There are two gardens, one behind the pub and one across the car park. Also across the car park is a large children's play area. Food ranges from sandwiches, jacket potatoes and salads to steaks and home-made pies and casseroles, with daily specials. There is a barbecue on Fridays and Saturdays in the summer and a Sunday carvery.

Telephone: 01626 360731.

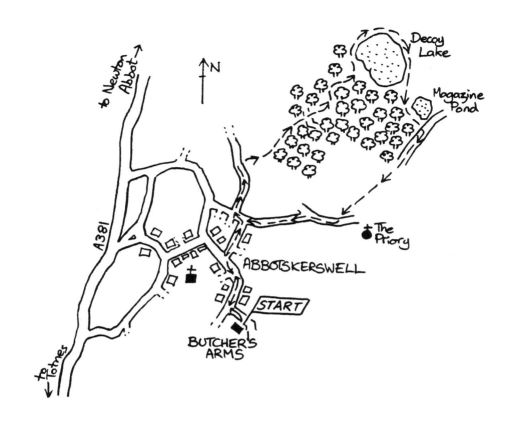

How to get there: Abbotskerswell is just off the A381 Newton Abbot to Totnes road. The turn-off is about 1¼ miles from Newton Abbot and is signposted. From the turn-off, follow the road as it winds through the village, until you come to a roundabout. Turn right here (signposted to Marldon and Paignton). The Butcher's Arms is a few hundred yards down this road on the right.

Parking: The pub has a large car park. Parking is difficult in the road, but the landlord has no objection to customers leaving their cars in the car park while walking, provided they ask.

10

Length of the walk: 3 miles. Maps: OS Explorer 110 Torquay and Dawlish; OS Landranger 202 Torbay and South Dartmoor area (GR 858685).

This pleasant, undemanding walk combines lanes and farm paths with woodland and lakeside trails, with a bit of nature study thrown in, and one superb viewpoint.

The Walk

From the pub, follow the road you drove in on back to the round-about. Turn right (signposted to Aller and Kingskerswell) and follow the lane up the hill. Near the top, where it curves to the right, turn left into Manor Road and immediately right into Stoneman's Hill. This takes you out of the village, still climbing slightly. About ¼ mile after leaving the village, you will find a stile through the hedge on your right and a public footpath sign.

Cross the stile into a field and start off by following the hedge on your right. When the hedge ends, do not follow the fence which veers off to the right but cut straight up the hill in front of you to the signpost at the top. The views from here are marvellous – to the north you can see Dartmoor and to the south the farmland rolling away almost as far as the sea.

Follow the direction of the signpost down the other side of the hill to the corner of the woods. Cross a stile and follow the path along the edge of the field, with the woods on your right. Cross the stile at the bottom, then the track in front of you, to enter Decoy woods.

A short distance into the woods, the path forks. Ignore the public footpath sign which points up to the right, and take the left-hand path, which is unsignposted. This leads you round the base of a small hill, with light and airy silver birch woodland stretching up the slope to your right and a dense marsh to your left. The whole area is a haven for birds, so if you are an ornithologist, bring your binoculars.

Once you have rounded the hill you will come to another fork. Take the left-hand path, which leads you down between two very muddy channels to a footbridge. Turn right over the bridge, and follow the wide path with a stream on the right and a wire fence on the left. The woods here are oak and beech rather than silver birch, and give a delightful variety of light and shade effects.

When you come to a break in the fence, turn sharp left to join the path which goes round Decoy Lake. This lake was once a china clay quarry, but it and the woods around it are now a popular recreational area for the people of Newton Abbot. The local council has made a very good job of reconciling the different needs of wildlife, walkers, anglers, water sports enthusiasts and families with young children. There is sailing on the lake in winter and windsurfing and canoeing in the summer. It is home to a variety of wildfowl, including moorhens, coots, swans, Canada geese, mallards and the ubiquitous gulls, and also plays host to a number of seasonal and occasional visitors.

Follow the path as it curves round to the right. As you go, you will see posts beside the path from time to time, showing the footprints of the various birds and animals that frequent the lake and woods. There are also various pieces of apparatus for the energetic, on which you can do sit-ups, pull-ups, step-ups, chin-ups and a variety of other strenuous exercises. Look out, too, for the beautiful wooden benches carved with designs created by local children.

Ignore the odd paths you will see leading off to the left and keep to the main track, which continues to curve to the right. You will catch occasional glimpses of the lake itself through the trees. When you have gone about three-quarters of the way round, the woods open up and you come out on to a grassy area, with picnic tables and a slipway for boats. From here you can get a good view of the lake and the woods behind it in all their beauty. It is a pretty sight at any time, but in the autumn, when the leaves are turning, it is particularly lovely.

A little way from the head of the slipway, you will find a notice board giving interesting information about the lake and its wildlife. There is also a kiosk, and further along a children's play area and paddling pool. The path goes on round, across the slipway, and just beyond the paddling pool it forks. Take the left-hand fork, which goes round to the right of some playing fields. You will find another picnic area beyond the wooden fence on the right. Go up to the higher field at the far end, and then turn right through a wooden fence. The small pond here is called Magazine Pond, and is another haven for waterbirds.

At the top of the steps beyond Magazine Pond, turn left down a broad path. After a short distance you cross a stile on to a farm track. Turn right and at the top, where the track ends, go straight on over a stile (signposted 'Public footpath'). The path runs along the edge of a field, at the end of which there is another stile. Cross it and keep left, skirting the next field. Cross a footbridge and yet another stile on your left and make your way diagonally across the next field to the last stile, which is in the hedge just to the right of a shed. Go right across the next field to a gateway which leads into a lane.

Turn right and follow the lane back to Abbotskerswell. At the roundabout at the bottom of the hill, turn left and retrace your route back to the pub.

② Beesands
The Cricket Inn

Beesands is an uncompromising old fishing village – a row of mainly pebble-dash fishermen's cottages strung along the shore, facing the elements head-on. And the Cricket is very much the village pub; there is very little to distinguish it from the other buildings apart from the sign. It is, however, a warm and welcoming place inside.

There is just the one room, divided into a panelled bar with a wooden floor and a carpeted dining area. It is decorated with old photographs of the village and examples of knotwork, and there is an open fire. Benches are provided out at the front by the sea wall. The food is very good, and ranges from the usual light meals to a wide range of local seafood. They also serve teas.

Telephone: 01548 580215.

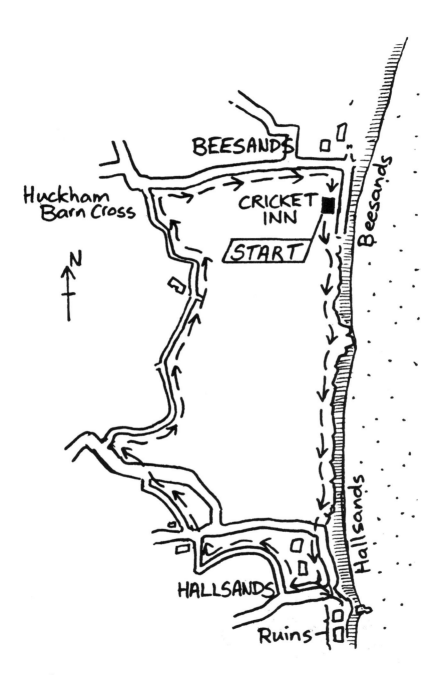

BEESANDS

Huckham
Barn Cross

CRICKET
INN

START

N

Beesands

Hallsands

HALLSANDS

Ruins

14

How to get there: The village is on the coast south of Torcross, and is clearly signposted from the A379 Torcross to Kingsbridge road. When you get to the village, turn right along the sea front to find the pub.

Parking: The pub has no car park, but free public parking is available across the road. There is also a free car park by the green, as you come into the village.

Length of the walk: 4¼ miles. Maps: OS Explorer OL20 South Devon; OS Landranger 202 Torbay and South Dartmoor area (GR 819404).

Follow the coast to the ruined fishing village of Hallsands, with glorious views but few gruelling climbs, and then meander back across fields and along quiet lanes and tracks, with hedgerows full of flowers and birds. Stout shoes or boots are recommended, and trousers rather than shorts are a must. Some of the tracks can be very muddy, and some of the paths are rather overgrown.

The Walk

Follow the sea-front road to the right outside the pub, and at the end bear right (signposted 'Coast Path Hallsands') to climb behind the houses and go through a gate to the clifftop. The views along the coast here stretch all the way back across the sands to Coombe Point, near Dartmouth, and to the lighthouse at Start Point ahead of you. Banks separate you from the cliff on the left and fields on the right, and this stretch is a haven for wild flowers.

After about ½ mile, you go through another gate and the path begins to descend, passing between high hedges and then emerging through two more gates at the beach at Hallsands. Cross the pebble beach and at the far end follow the tarred road (signposted 'Coast Path Start Point'). At the end turn right (signposted 'Coast Path') and follow the path round to the left behind some buildings, first up some steps and then down some more, passing a group of houses on the right. At the end of the row are Trouts holiday apartments. Just beyond Trouts on the rocks below are the remains of the old fishing village of Hallsands. Unfortunately you can no longer go down to them, as the path has collapsed.

These stark ruins, all that remain of a flourishing community, are a poignant reminder of the power of the sea. After withstanding the elements for 300 years, the village was washed away by violent storms in January 1917. The cause is not known for certain, but a contributory factor seems to have been the dredging of sand and shingle from the sea bed just off shore. There was a certain amount of damage to the village in the early years of last century, and dredging ceased as a result. But whether the undermining of the sea bed led directly to the village's final destruction or simply accelerated a process that would have taken its toll eventually anyway, no one seems to know.

Turn right into the lane that runs alongside Trouts. Follow it past some tennis courts and a putting green on the left. A few yards beyond the putting green, you will find a gate and stile on the right (signposted 'Public footpath Bickerton'). Cross the field beyond to a fence, pausing to admire the view along the coast to Coombe Point again. Do not go through the gate immediately in front of you, but keep the fence on your right to another gate leading on to a track.

The track passes between hedges and curves to the left to join a lane. Turn right along the lane (signposted 'Public footpath') and follow it past a farm. Where it joins another lane, cross straight over to a track (signposted 'Higher Bickerton Lane, public bridleway'). This track becomes a bit overgrown and can be a little muddy, but it is quite passable. It leads down to another lane, where you turn left.

After about 200 yards, the lane curves sharply to the left. Turn right here on to a track (signposted 'Public byway Higher Middlecombe'). The track curves first to the right and then to the left, climbing as it goes. There is a marvellous variety of hedgerow plants along here, and plenty of birds.

You pass through a gate and continue up to Higher Middlecombe Farm. It gets very muddy along here in wet weather. At the farm, go through a gate, turn left and bear right through another gate, following the red arrows.

The path emerges into a lane. Turn right for a short climb followed by some lovely views as you reach the top of the hill. The lane then runs down to Huckham Barn Cross, where it joins another lane. Turn right (signposted to Beesands). After a little over ½ mile you will come to a junction. Go straight on to Beesands and turn right along the sea front to return to the pub.

3 **West Charleton**
The Ashburton Arms

West Charleton is an attractive village just inland from the Kingsbridge Estuary, a nature reserve and part of the South Devon Area of Outstanding Natural Beauty. It is an ideal starting point for an exploration of this delightful area.

The Ashburton Arms is on the main road through the village. It is an old farmhouse, once part of the estate of the Barons Ashburton – hence the name. It is a warm, welcoming place, comprising a long bar, with beer mugs and foreign bank notes adorning the low beams and old photographs on the walls. It has small leaded windows and there is an open fire at one end. Through an archway at the other end is a beautifully furnished restaurant. There are also tables outside where you can sit and watch the village go about its business on a sunny day.

The food is very varied, ranging from baguettes, ploughman's lunches, scampi and their renowned steak on the rocks (a variety of steaks served on hot granite rocks) at midday to a full restaurant menu in the evenings. There are also daily specials.

Telephone: 01548 531242.

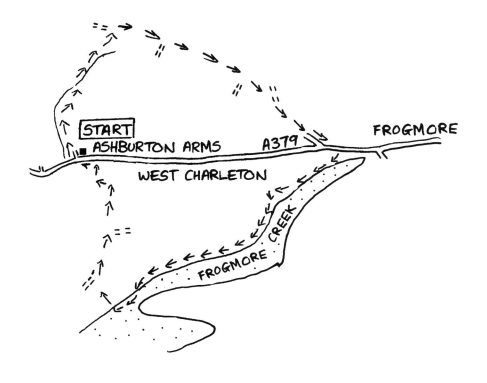

How to get there: West Charleton is on the A379 Kingsbridge to Dartmouth road, just east of Kingsbridge. The pub is on the main road.

Parking: The pub has a large car park, and the landlord has no objection to customers leaving their cars there while they walk, as long as they ask. There is also parking in the side road which runs alongside the pub.

Length of the walk: 4¼ miles. Maps: OS Explorer OL20 South Devon; OS Landranger 202 Torbay and South Dartmoor area (GR 752426).

Two of the most attractive features of this part of South Devon are the network of green lanes that criss-cross the area, providing homes for a wide variety of animals, birds and flowers, and the estuaries, creeks and inlets that spread their tentacles inland from the coast. This pretty walk takes full advantage of both. On the way out you follow green lanes to the nearby village of Frogmore, and the return leg is along Frogmore Creek, part of the Salcombe and Kingsbridge Estuary Nature Reserve. The going is generally easy, although there are one or two muddy stretches.

The Walk

Turn right along the A379, and after 50 yards or so, just after the pavement ends, turn right up a path, following the public footpath sign. You emerge onto a drive; bear left and then, at the T-junction, turn right. When you reach the gate to a house called Leat Head, go through a kissing-gate just to the right of it, following the yellow waymark. A path takes you between a hedge and a fence to another gate. Keep to the left of the field on the other side. At the end are four gates, two to the left and two ahead of you: climb slightly up the hill on the right to the fourth, which is marked with a yellow waymark.

Keep to the left of the next field, and at the end go through a small gate and across a stone stile. Keep to the left again and then swing left to cross the stream alongside you. On the other side is a path junction; bear right to continue along the other bank of the stream rather than heading directly up the hill. Cross a stile and keep to the right of the next field. Cross a stone stile at the other end into a green lane.

Turn right and follow the lane as it climbs steadily, crossing a small stream as you go. After about ¼ mile you will come to a junction, with another green lane going off to the right; go straight on. Soon afterwards, the green lane levels off and after 600 yards you will come to another junction, with a path going left and another green lane going right. Go straight on again, but as you do so look to the right for a superb view down Frogmore Creek to the Kingsbridge Estuary and the sea. Another ¼ mile brings you to a T-junction; turn right and follow another green lane downhill through a tunnel of trees. You come out onto a lane in the village of Frogmore; follow that down to the main road.

Turn left and follow the road for about 150 yards to a wooden public footpath sign pointing between two houses on the right (take care, because it is a busy road and there is no pavement along here). Turn right (signposted to Frogmore Creek and West Charleton) and go through a gate. Keep to the left of a field and at the bottom turn right to follow the hedge round. Cross a stone stile and follow the path between two fences. You now have Frogmore Creek on your left. Part of the Salcombe and Kingsbridge Nature Reserve, it is a haven for water birds. After a while you cross a wooden stile and then a V-stile, and bear right across a field. At the path junction at the end, go left (signposted to Geese Quarries). Cross two stone stiles and go through a gate. You are now back alongside the creek and you can see an old lime kiln on the other bank. You cross four V-stiles, keeping alongside the creek all the while. At the end of the last field you cross a small stream and then after a while the path takes you down to the creek shore. Turn right and follow the shoreline for about 200 yards.

Leave the creek via a track, following the public footpath sign. It climbs up the bank through some trees, and as it emerges you get a good view ahead over West Charleton and the rolling South Hams countryside. You join another track; go straight on. When this track swings right, go straight on through a gate, following the public footpath sign. Cut straight across a field, and on the other side turn left. After 100 yards turn right through a gap in the hedge and cross a stile. Keep right in the next field to a kissing-gate and follow a surfaced path up to the main road. Turn left, and you will find the Ashburton Arms on your right about 150 yards along the road.

Bovey Tracey
The Old Thatched Inn

Bovey Tracey is a pleasant town, worth a visit in its own right, and a useful centre for exploring the south-eastern corner of Dartmoor. Of particular interest is the shop and exhibition centre of the Devon Guild of Craftsmen, which is about 50 yards from the pub. You can spend a happy hour or so browsing there among the work of local craftsmen of all kinds, from potters and blacksmiths to needleworkers and carpenters.

The Old Thatched Inn is an attractive 17th century thatched coaching inn and has been very well preserved and decorated, retaining its traditional charm. There is a delightful bar, with a dining room alongside and a large chimney in between, with stone fireplaces on both sides. The floor is also of stone and there are low oak beams. Off the bar is a games room, and there is a pleasant beer garden at the back.

The food is good, with a variety of bar snacks and main meals. Telephone: 01626 833421.

How to get there: Bovey Tracey is on the A382 between Newton Abbot and Moretonhampstead and about 2 miles from the A38. From the bypass, follow the signs to the town centre. The pub is on the right about 50 yards before the bridge.

Parking: There is a public car park just beyond the pub.

Length of the walk: 2½ miles. Maps: OS Explorer 110 Torquay and Dawlish; OS Landranger 191 Okehampton and North Dartmoor area (GR 813781).

The walk takes in Parke, a National Trust estate on the outskirts of Bovey Tracey, which also encompasses the headquarters of the Dartmoor National Park Authority. So there is a lot of interest on this gentle ramble, which follows the route of a dismantled railway through some lovely woods, and then brings you back along a charming riverside path.

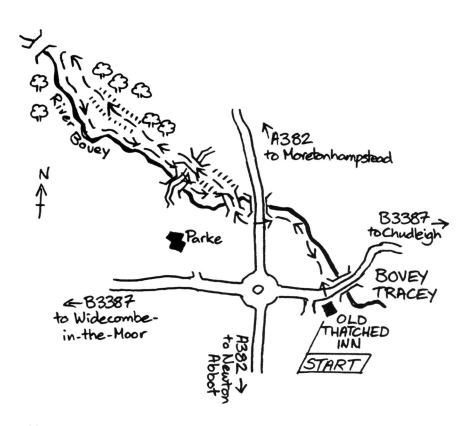

The Walk

Cross the road outside the pub and turn right. Follow the railings, and just before you reach the bridge, turn left into a park. It is a pleasant area, well planted with trees, and with the river Bovey running along the edge. You pass a children's play area and then a football pitch on the left, with the river still on the right. At the end of the football pitch is a kissing-gate leading on to the bypass.

Cross the road to another kissing-gate, which leads into the National Trusts's Parke Estate, and on to the track of a dismantled railway, once part of the line that linked Newton Abbot with the moors. Initially the river will still be on the right, but the track soon crosses a bridge, and the river disappears off to the left while the track goes straight on.

The trees form an arch overhead as you enter a beautiful deciduous wood, mainly of beech. The dappled light and shade effects caused by the sun filtering through the trees above can be quite magical, and there is birdsong all around. In spring, the path is edged with primroses.

Ignore the paths and tracks leading off to the left and right; just follow the line of the railway straight on. You pass under a fine,

Some of the glorious countryside near Bovey Tracey.

arched stone bridge, and then after another 300 yards the track divides into three. Take the left-hand branch, which leads down to the river, with a stand of conifers on the left.

The path curves to the left along the riverbank, with the conifers still on the left. It is delightful along here, with the sun making highlights on the water. You pass a bridge on the right, then go through two kissing-gates to enter deciduous woodland again, and you will soon come to a small sandy stretch of riverbank, almost like a beach. This is an ideal place to stop for a break and absorb the tranquil scene around you – there is even a bench to sit on. All that breaks the silence is the sound of the river as it tumbles over the rocks in front of you.

The path soon passes a weir and then crosses a footbridge over a ditch. About ¼ mile further on, there is a raised walkway; turn right beyond it and you come out into a field. Near the end, there is a stone bridge over the river on the right. Carry straight on past and over a footbridge. Go up the steps to the left and follow the path round the rocky outcrop above the river. Cross a stile into a field, still with the river on your right. At the end of the field cross a stile and climb the steps to the left to reach the dismantled railway. Turn right to retrace your steps along the railway and across the bypass to the park and back to the pub.

5 Bridford
The Bridford Inn

The Bridford Inn, which lies at the end of this attractive little village near the eastern edge of the Dartmoor National Park, has been in existence only about 35 years. It was originally a row of 17th century cottages, but has been extremely tastefully converted. There is one large bar, with a small family room off it. It still has the original bare stone walls in parts, and there are low beams and a large stone fireplace. The bar counter is interesting – wider than most, having originally been a chemist's counter. A small beer garden is sited at the front, between the pub and the car park.

The food is varied and interesting, ranging from bar snacks to steaks, chicken and vegetarian meals.

Telephone: 01647 252436.

How to get there: Bridford lies just north of Christow, about a mile west of the B3193 Teign Valley road, and it is signposted from that road. When you enter the village, turn left at the T-junction, and the pub is up a drive to the right a few hundred yards further on.

Parking: The pub has its own car park. Parking in the road is difficult, but the landlord will usually allow customers to leave their cars in the pub car park while walking if they ask permission first and park with consideration for others.

Length of the walk: 4½ miles. Maps: OS Explorer 110 Torquay and Dawlish; OS Landranger 191 Okehampton and North Dartmoor area (GR 813861).

Although Bridford is within the Dartmoor National Park, this is not a moorland walk. It takes you through some beautiful woods, across attractive farmland and alongside a lovely reservoir, with the option of extending it to take in further attractive waterside meanders.

The Walk

Go down the pub drive and turn right down the lane at the bottom, which soon becomes an unsurfaced track (signposted 'Public bridlepath'). This takes you down to a stream, with dense woodland on either side. The main track curves to the left to cross the stream, but you need to go straight on through the gate ahead of you (signposted 'Public footpath Laployd via Hedgemoor').

This new track leads you deeper into the woods, climbing as you go. It then curves to the left. Instead of following it, go straight on through a gate to a path. There is no signpost, but you cannot miss it, as it takes you alongside the stream, still climbing. This is a delightful stretch, with the stream tumbling down on your right and the cool green woods all around you.

At the top, the path opens up to a grassy track. A few yards along this track turn left, following the 'path' sign. The path curves up to the edge of the trees. Keep to the left of the newly planted area beyond and cross the bank at a yellow-painted post to reach a gate. Go through it and keep to the left of the field. Halfway across you will see a hedge stretching across to your right. Turn right beyond this hedge and follow it to a stile. Keep to the right of the field on the other side.

Go through the gate at the end, and follow the line of trees on your

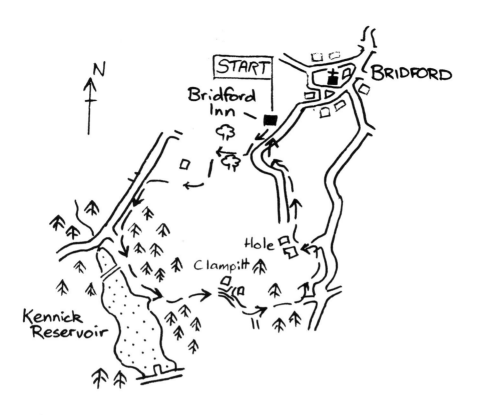

right to a gateway. Keep to the right of the next field, and cross the stile at the end into a lane. Turn left. After about 200 yards you will see the conifers of Laployd Plantation on your left and the lane will begin to descend. At the bottom, after another 500 yards, there is a track to the left, leading into the plantation, signposted to parking for Kennick anglers and a public bridlepath. Turn in here.

This is the beginning of Kennick Reservoir, the first of three linked reservoirs (the others are Tottiford and Trenchford). It is a lovely spot, with a variety of delightful walks alongside and around the water. As you enter the track, there is a notice board with a map showing the various routes that are open to you if you want to extend your walk at this stage. In spring, the rhododendrons are particularly splendid around these reservoirs.

Our route follows the bridlepath, with the conifer plantation on the left, Kennick Reservoir on the right and ahead, and wild flowers all around. In late summer, this area is a pink mass of rosebay willowherb.

Just beyond the sluice gates, bear left (signposted 'Bridlepath') and climb up among the trees, eventually losing sight of the reservoir. At the junction, go straight on (signposted 'Bridlepath to Clampitt Cottage'). The path is quite clear, but just to make sure you do not get lost, green arrows occasionally point the way. After a while you renew your acquaintance with the reservoir, with views down to it through the trees on your right.

The path soon curves left and leaves the plantation to skirt round to the right of a field (signposted 'Bridlepath to Clampitt Cottage'). It then curves to the right to enter a stretch of deciduous woodland, and meets a track. Turn right here (signposted 'Bridlepath Clampitt Cottage') and follow the track round to the left along the edge of a wood until you come to a gateway and another track.

Turn left at this track (both directions say simply 'Bridlepath'). Just beyond the farm barn on the left, there is a junction. Go straight on (signposted 'Bridlepath county road for Christow'). This stretch is a mass of rhododendrons, and is gorgeous in the spring. The surface becomes progressively better as you follow the track down, from unsurfaced to roughly surfaced to tarred.

When you reach the road, turn left (signposted to Bridford). There are pleasant views to the right along this road, and soon Bridford comes into view ahead of you as the road dips. At Middle Hole Farm, turn left through the gate and follow the drive round to a small gate to the right of the house, marked 'Bridlepath'.

Go up the left-hand side of the field beyond to another gate. Turn right and follow a path between trees to another farm. Go through the farmyard and on to the track on the other side, with rolling views to the right. At the bottom, cross the stream and you will find yourself on the track you started on. Turn right and make your way back to the pub.

⑥ Chagford
The Ring o' Bells

Chagford is an ancient stannary town, where the tin-miners of Dartmoor used to bring their tin to be assessed and weighed, and where offenders against the miners' laws were tried. It is a pretty little place – more like a village in size and atmosphere than a town – with pleasant shops clustered around the Square, and four pubs, all within a couple of hundred yards of each other.

The pubs all have their attractions, but the Ring o' Bells is my personal choice for charm and atmosphere. The present building dates back about 300 years, but there has been an inn on the site since the 12th century. It has a long and somewhat varied history. The stannary court used to be held here and the back part was used as a holding prison for prisoners on their way to Okehampton Assizes. Also at the back was the town morgue.

There is a long bar at the front, full of character and divided by partitions and screens to form a series of semi alcoves. It is decorated with old photographs and prints, and there is an open fire in winter. Behind the bar is the Stannary Buttery, an attractively decorated and furnished dining area, and at the back of the pub is the beer garden, a pretty courtyard with flower-beds and an arbour.

29

There is a varied and very interesting menu, ranging from sandwiches to main meals.

Telephone: 01647 432466.

How to get there: Chagford lies north-west of Moretonhampstead, about 1¼ miles from the A382 and is clearly signposted from that road. Follow the road into the town until you reach a T-junction at the Square and High Street. The Ring o' Bells is just to the left across High Street.

Parking: The pub has no car park. If you cannot find parking in the road outside, there is a large pay and display public car park about 150 yards up the road past the church.

Length of the walk: 4 miles. Maps: OS Explorer OL28 Dartmoor; OS Landranger 191 Okehampton and North Dartmoor area (GR 700875).

This is a delightfully varied walk, taking in a bit of moorland, a bit of woodland and a riverside path. It is generally undemanding, except for one short climb near the start, and some excellent views can be enjoyed.

The Walk

Turn right outside the pub. As you walk along High Street, you will pass the Three Crowns Hotel, in the porch of which the poet and ardent Royalist Sidney Godolphin died, somewhat dramatically and romantically, after being shot in battle in the Civil War.

At the end of High Street, turn right into New Street (signposted to Postbridge). This is a narrow street of attractive stone houses, with the great bulk of Meldon Hill looming to the right. As you near the edge of the town, almost ½ mile from the centre, take the road turning off to the left (it is in fact the first turning you come to on the left). After about 150 yards, look for a path leading off to the left between two houses (signposted to Nattadon Common).

Take this path and climb to a copse. Cross a stile. The sign indicating the direction you want (Nattadon) points half-right from the stile, but the path actually goes right and then left. It continues to wind right

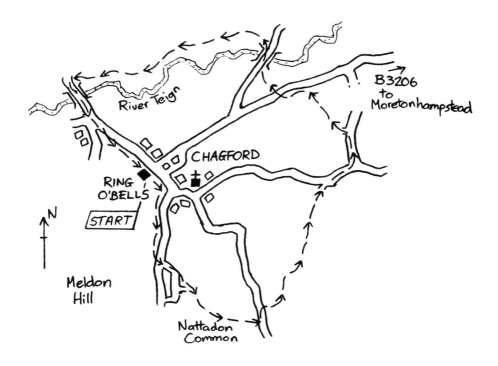

and left and then climbs straight up the hill through the bracken to Nattadon Common, parallel to the trees on the left, but about 50 yards from them. There is a lovely view backwards, with Meldon Hill in the foreground, then farms and woods, and the open moorland of Chagford Common, Gidleigh Common and Throwleigh Common in the distance.

Towards the top of the hill, you meet a fence on your left. Bear right and follow this fence. As you breast the hill, more superb views open up to the left. At the end of the fence is a small grassed parking area which leads into a lane. Turn left and then after a few yards right over a stile (signposted 'Footpath road Great Weeke'). Cross to another stile, then turn left and follow the hedge. As you do so, you can see all the way to Castle Drogo, perched dramatically above the gorge of the river Teign ahead of you.

At the end of the field, cross a stile and keep to the left-hand side of the next field to some trees at the end. There is a very attractive path leading through the trees between two walls to a gate. Go through the gate and continue along the track, with massive old oaks on either side and a wide variety of wild flowers all around.

The track descends steeply to a lane. Turn right here and pass two attractive thatched stone houses on the left. Take the lane which leads off to the left just past them (signposted 'Adley Lane'). After about 200 yards you will find a track leading off to the left. Follow it to a stile and a public footpath sign.

Cross the stile and go diagonally across the field on the other side to another stile. Cross the next field diagonally to cross a third stile on to a path between some houses. This leads to yet another stile and a lane. Go straight ahead down the lane to reach the road into Chagford. Turn left here and then right across a stile after about 50 yards.

Bear left along the edge of the field to a stile into a lane. Turn right to cross Rushford Bridge and then left into a field through a gate. Once in the field, head for the centre of the hedge on your right. Go through the gap and across to a footbridge over a leat, followed by a gate. Go through and straight on (signposted 'Chagford Bridge'), with the tree-lined leat on the left and a field on the right. This stretch is a mass of bluebells in the spring, and if you enjoy making your own wine it is a good place to come for elderberries in September and October.

Go through the next gate into another field and cross a stile at the end into a copse. You soon come to the river Teign and the weir where the leat leads off. Go through a gate into a field, and at the end cross a footbridge, which is followed by a gate and another footbridge. You soon pass through yet another gate into another field. It is beautifully peaceful along here, with the river flowing quietly by on your left and meadows on your right.

The path goes through another gate into another field. Notice how the oaks along here appear to be on stone platforms. This is presumably because they were originally part of a hedge on a bank which was subsequently removed. You then come to a wall and fence on the left and go down to a gate. Cross the next field to another gate, which leads into a lane.

Turn left and cross the old packhorse bridge. After a couple of hundred yards you will come to a crossroads. Turn left (signposted to Chagford) and follow the road up into the town. At the junction, go straight on into High Street and back to the Ring o' Bells on the right.

Dartington
The White Hart

The White Hart is part of the magnificent medieval Dartington Hall, built in the 14th century by John Holand, half-brother of Richard II. The Hall comprises a collection of lovingly restored stone buildings around an attractive courtyard.

Set in one corner of the courtyard, and as pleasing inside as it is outside, the White Hart has a fairly small, cosy bar, with a flagstoned floor and an open fire to one side. Off the bar is a large, high-ceilinged dining room. There are also some tables on a patio outside, looking out onto the superb gardens.

The food on offer ranges from soup and baguettes to such delights as roast pheasant breast and red mullet. Wherever possible, it is locally sourced and organic. There is also a range of organic drinks.

Telephone: 01803 847111.

How to get there: Either turn north off the A385 Totnes to Plymouth road just outside Totnes or turn east off the A384 Dartington to

Buckfastleigh road just north of Dartington. In both cases a drive leads straight to Dartington Hall. The White Hart is in the far left-hand corner of the courtyard.

Parking: There is a small car park opposite the massive wooden gates leading into the courtyard and a larger one a few yards along the drive to the west.

Length of the walk: 2¾ miles (although an exploration of the Dartington Hall gardens will make it a bit longer). Maps: OS Explorer 110 Torquay and Dawlish or OL20 South Devon; OS Landranger 202 Torbay and South Dartmoor (GR 799626).

The highlight of this undemanding walk is an exploration of Dartington Hall and its beautiful gardens, but it also takes in a delightful riverside stroll and the chance – by going slightly out of your way – to do a bit of shopping! Dogs are not allowed in the Hall courtyard or gardens, but if you have one a short detour can be made along the drive.

The Walk

The route description starts at the gates to the Hall courtyard. If you have a dog, you should turn right as you face the gates and follow the drive as it winds and curves round the hall and gardens until you come to a public footpath sign pointing into a field on the left.

Otherwise go through the gates into the courtyard. The Hall is now a conference and educational centre, and headquarters of the Dartington Hall Trust, a charitable organisation set up by the last owners, Dorothy and Leonard Elmhirst, to promote their two great passions – educational innovation and rural regeneration. The buildings on each side of the courtyard are not open to the public, but the Great Hall at the end can be visited when it is not in use, and it is well worth seeing, with its enormous vaulted ceiling and high windows. Note the banners along the walls, which symbolise the various activities in which the Trust is engaged.

To the left of the Great Hall is the White Hart. To get to the gardens go round to the left. If you follow the path round, keeping the White Hart and the Great Hall on your right all the time, you will come out at the amphitheatre, a superb terraced area, once used for jousting tournaments, which provides a good focal point. There are paths to follow in all directions, with a heather garden one way, a lovely collection of azaleas and rhododendrons another, a water garden, a meadow and a majestic collection of trees all around you. The gardens are beautiful in all seasons, but in my view the very best times to visit are spring, when all the most colourful flowers and

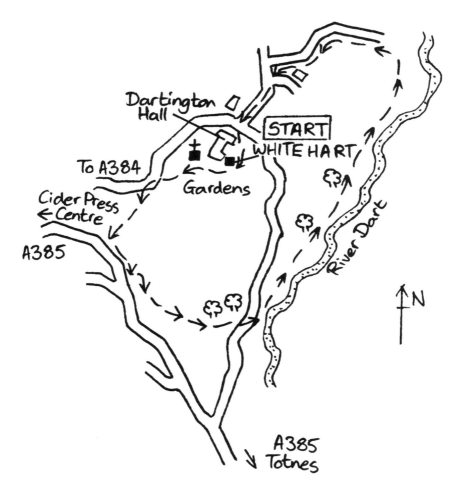

Dartington Hall

START

WHITE HART

To A384

Gardens

Cider Press Centre

A385

River Dart

↑N

A385 Totnes

blossoms are out, and autumn, when the rich variety of foliage colours is breathtaking.

When you have had your fill, aim for the far right-hand corner of the gardens as you look across the amphitheatre from the wall in front of the Great Hall. There you will find a gate into the drive. Turn left outside the gate, and after a few yards left again to go through a gate into a field (signposted 'Public footpath').

Keep to the right-hand side of the field, following the hedge to a stile at the end. Cross into the next field and follow the hedge on the left to the next stile, which leads to a track. Go straight down the track for about 50 yards until you come to a stile on the right. Cross into another field and turn left, heading towards the wood on the other side. Cross a stile into the wood and go down a short path, which joins another at right angles. Turn right here and go down to the riverside path at the bottom.

If you want to make a detour here you can turn right and follow the path to the Cider Press Centre. This houses an excellent collection of shops where you can browse through craft work, gifts, Dartington glass, kitchenware, books, toys, plants and foodstuffs. If you do not want to visit the Cider Press Centre, turn sharp left alongside the riverside path. Where it forks after about 150 yards, take the left fork. Soon you cross a set of cattle grids. Stretching up the hill on the left is a wood of mainly oak and beech, while on the right is Queen's Meadow, a floodplain which is a haven for a variety of water birds, especially swans, ducks and gulls. Pass through the gate at the end of the path, and turn left to follow the drive up to the Hall. You can see the River Dart down on your right as you go, and soon you leave the drive to go down to it.

Ignore the first path you come to, which goes off to the right at right angles to the drive, but take the next one, which goes half-right, over a stile and across a field to a small copse by the river. At the end of the copse you cross a meadow. It is lovely along here, with the green meadow to the left and the river flowing slowly and placidly along to the right, flanked by oaks, beeches and sycamores. In summer, this whole stretch of riverbank is a mass of Himalayan balsam, with its beautifully shaped, delicate pink flowers and large, bright green leaves.

Cross a stile into a patch of woodland, and then a second into another meadow, still with the same combination of oak, beech, sycamore and (in summer) Himalayan balsam along the bank to your right. When you come to a concrete track leading out of the meadow to the left, turn up it. You pass some school grounds on your left and then a plain white building. Immediately beyond it, turn left up some steps over a bank. Turn right in the drive and then right again. At the T-junction at the top, turn left to follow the road a few hundred yards to the Hall entrance.

8 Denbury
The Union Inn

Village greens are fairly rare in Devon, but at Denbury we have something even rarer – a village green that is hardly in the village at all. Here the green is not the traditional hub of the village; it is at the very edge, with just a couple of houses and the pub alongside it.

The Union is a 17th century inn, fairly plain outside, but most attractive inside, with low beams, bare stone walls and four lovely old stone fireplaces. The main bar is U-shaped and full of horse brasses and other knick-knacks, and there are two delightful, cosy rooms off to the side, decorated with old paintings of country scenes. There is also a patio at the back with benches and tables.

The pub has won awards for its impressive food, which ranges from bar snacks to an array of main courses, including Devon specialities, steaks and seafood.

Telephone: 01803 812595.

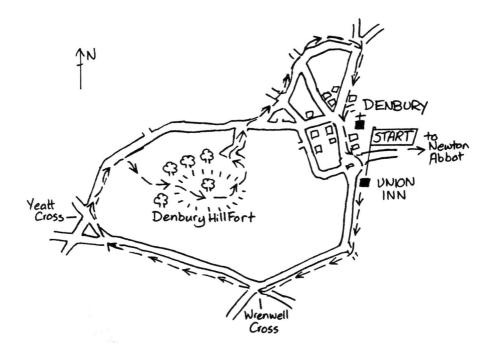

How to get there: Denbury is about 2½ miles from Newton Abbot. Follow the signs from the A381 Newton Abbot to Totnes road, passing through East Ogwell on the way. The pub is on the left of the village green just before you enter the village proper.

Parking: There are only a few parking spaces immediately outside the pub, but you should be able to find parking round the green.

Length of the walk: 3 miles. Maps: OS Explorer 110 Torquay and Dawlish; OS Landranger 202 Torbay and South Dartmoor area (GR 824686).

This is a delightful undemanding walk almost all along quiet country lanes. For those interested in history there is a visit to the site of the Devonians' last stand against the invading Saxons, for those who appreciate the rolling Devon hills there are some lovely views, and for everyone there are pretty and varied hedgerows.

38

The Walk

Take the lane that leads off to the left of the green, round the corner of the pub. Follow it for about ½ mile to Wrenwell Cross. Turn right (signposted to Woodland and Ashburton). This is a good stretch for picking blackberries in late summer, and there are excellent views ahead and to the left, across a patchwork of fields to the moors in the distance.

At the next crossroads, turn right again (signposted to Denbury and Newton Abbot). The view to the left is still superb, and you can clearly see Haytor etched against the skyline. After about 300 yards, the lane makes an S-bend. In the middle of the S, look for a black gate on the right. There is no public footpath sign, but there is a stile alongside it and, if you look up the hill towards the woods above you will see another gate with a stile alongside it.

Cross the stile and go up the field to the second one. Cross it and enter the wood, which is mainly of beech, oak and chestnut and is a delightful place at any time, but especially in spring and autumn. There is a moderate climb up to a gate which leads into Denbury Hill Fort, a massive defensive system covering some 9½ acres. It was here that the Devonians were finally defeated by the Saxon King Centwine in AD 681, an event that is reflected in the village's name – it is a corruption of Defnasburh, meaning 'the fortified place of the Devonians'.

The hill fort is now covered in trees, which are lovely to stroll through, but which make it difficult to imagine what the site must have been like in those far-off days. However, the path meanders between two large tumuli, ancient burial mounds that are clearly visible, and just before the gate at the end there is a path leading off to the right which follows the line of the fort's defences. These consisted of the traditional agger (a raised causeway) and fosse (a trench 19 ft deep), as well as a stronger external defence, all of which can still be seen. You can follow the path a short way to get some idea of what it might have been like crouching beneath these massive earthworks waiting for the Saxons to attack, but it soon becomes too overgrown to continue, and you have to retrace your steps.

Where the path along the defences leaves the main route, there is a superb view over Denbury to the rolling fields and hills stretching away to the east. Follow the main path to the gate leading out of the hill fort and then follow the track beyond, still with those lovely views across the hills ahead and to the right. The track winds down to rejoin the lane. Turn right here and then immediately left down Denbury Down Lane.

At the crossroads, go straight on down a narrow lane, and at the next crossroads straight on down a track. Do *not* follow the public footpath sign pointing half-left across a field. Our track is a medieval route for bypassing the village. It is a pleasant byway running between attractive hedges, but it can become a bit muddy in wet weather.

At the end, just before it emerges onto a lane, you will see a gate leading to a paved path on the right. Go through and follow the path between hedges until it comes out alongside the lane, then follow the lane into Denbury. Much of the housing in the village is pretty uninspiring, but the centre is still very attractive. At the old water conduit at the crossroads in the centre, turn left (signposted to Ipplepen and Newton Abbot). As you walk back towards the green along this road, you pass a high wall, behind which are the remains of the cell of a local monk called Aeldred, who rose to become Archbishop of York and crowned both Edward the Confessor and William the Conqueror.

9 East Ogwell
The Jolly Sailor

How does a pub in a mainly agricultural area, many miles from the sea, come to be called the Jolly Sailor? That was the question that immediately came to mind when I first visited this beautiful old cob-walled and thatched inn. The answer lies in the days when press gangs roamed the country looking for men to press into the navy. The gangs from Plymouth came to Newton Abbot, but did not get as far as sleepy little Ogwell, so that is where the sailors of the area did their drinking, safe from the rigours of naval service.

Although it was given its present name in 1898, the pub dates back to the late 18th century and the building to 1510. It was originally three cottages, built to house the workers building the church across the road. This history was reflected in the pub's original name, the Church House Inn.

It is a delightful place, full of character and a great favourite with locals. It comprises a long bar, with low black beams, an enormous fireplace at one end and a games area, with pool and darts, in an alcove at the other. Through the bar is a most attractive little restaurant and out at the back a pleasant garden.

The food is excellent, and the pub prides itself on the fact that the dishes are all home-made. These range from bar snacks to wholesome main meals such as steaks and seafood.

Telephone: 01626 354581.

How to get there: East Ogwell is just outside Newton Abbot, and is best approached from the roundabout on the A381 Totnes road just on the outskirts of the town, from which it is signposted. Follow the road to Ogwell Green, where you fork right (signposted to East Ogwell and West Ogwell). The pub is at the bottom of the hill on the left.

Parking: There is a large car park alongside the pub. The landlord has no objection to customers leaving their cars there while they walk.

Length of the walk: 3 miles. Maps: OS Explorer 110 Torquay and Dawlish; OS Landranger 202 Torbay and South Dartmoor area (GR 838700).

This route takes you to Bradley Woods, and a lovely stretch of woodland and riverbank, with some interesting places to see along the way. It is beautiful at any time, but especially so in spring, when the woods are carpeted with wild flowers. It is an undemanding amble, with just two fairly easy climbs.

The Walk

On leaving the pub, head right, back the way you came, and climb the short hill to the green. Bear left here, following the direction of the footpath sign across the green to a stile. Cross it and keep to the right of the field on the other side to another stile. Keep to the left of the next field. There are good views all around you, with the unmistakable outline of Haytor to the left and Newton Abbot and the Teign estuary to the right.

Go down the hill and into Bradley Woods to a stile on the left. Cross it and follow the path down the hill, deeper into the woods. At the bottom, turn left, following the 'public footpath' sign. You climb some steps and follow the path as it runs above the river Lemon. Climb some more steps and cross a stile. Soon you will see Puritans' Pit on your right. It is an interesting place, and worth exploring; there are steps leading down to the bottom. Its origins are somewhat

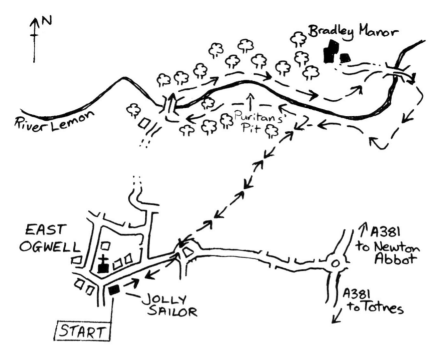

obscure – some people believe that it is an old quarry, others a collapsed cavern. It derives its name from the fact that it was a meeting place for nonconformists when they were being persecuted. The Revd William Yeo used to preach there.

Just beyond the pit, the path widens. This is a delightful piece of woodland, with beech, hawthorn, rowan and a variety of other trees, and the slope on the left is a mass of bluebells in the spring.

Soon you will go through a kissing-gate and then leave the wood through another gate. The path curves right and then left and then right again to cross the river by a footbridge. Turn right and go through a kissing-gate, then across a track and through another kissing-gate into a field, with the river on your right.

At the end of the field, go through a gate. The river curves away to the right over a weir, while the path runs alongside a leat leading off it, which used to serve Bradley Mill. It re-enters the woods, which are still quite varied, but now mainly beech. In spring, the area on the left, opposite the leat, is white with wild garlic flowers.

You soon cross the leat and rejoin the river, walking between the two, and go through a gateway into a meadow which abounds with wild flowers of different kinds throughout the year. The meadow narrows and then widens out again, and you will find Bradley Manor on your left. This is a medieval manor house now owned by the National Trust. It is a very interesting building and well worth a visit, especially the kitchens and the chapel.

Here the path is tarred, as it forms the drive to Bradley Manor. It curves to the right, away from the leat to cross the river by a stone bridge. Immediately after the bridge, turn right. Cross a footbridge, go through a kissing-gate and along the right-hand side of a field to another kissing-gate to enter the woods again.

Go straight on, along the banks of the river, and follow it round to the right. The sun filtering through the trees dapples the path and the water, creating some magical effects. You will come to a path leading off to the left; ignore it and carry straight on past a footbridge on the right. Soon you will come to another path leading off to the left, this time marked by a public footpath sign. Take this one to climb back up the way you came originally. At the fork, go right, cross the stile at the top and go right again.

You now leave the woods. Keep to the right of the field ahead to the stile, and keep to the left of the next field to the last stile. This leads out on to Ogwell Green, where you bear right to join the lane and go back down to the village and the Jolly Sailor.

Harberton
The Church House Inn

Harberton is a lovely, unspoilt village of stone cottages and farm-houses set in a valley, and with a beautiful old church next door to the pub which is worth a visit – the 14th century screen is particularly fine.

The Church House Inn is a gem of a pub in a gem of a village. It was built originally to house the men working on the church alongside in the 12th century, and you can still see a latticed window dating back to the 13th century, with some of the original glass in it – one of the oldest pieces of ecclesiastical glass in the country. There is also some superb medieval oak panelling.

The pub is a long building set right on the village square, with a magnificent old stone fireplace at one end, now containing a wood-burning stove. On either side of the fireplace are two delightful little nooks. Despite its size, the bar has a warm, cosy atmosphere, which is enhanced by the massive beams, thick stone walls and small windows that are typical of the period. It is furnished with beautiful old settles and tables and chairs, and the floor is carpeted at one end and tiled at the other – ideal for people with muddy boots after their walk.

An attractive family room leads off the bar at the opposite end from the fireplace. Although there is no garden as such, there are benches outside on the square for those who want to sit in the sun and survey the life of the village.

The food can be highly recommended. It ranges from sandwiches and ploughman's lunches to steaks and a range of other mouthwatering main courses.

Telephone: 01803 863707.

How to get there: Harberton is about 3 miles from Totnes, just off the A381 Totnes to Kingsbridge road, from which it is signposted. Do not confuse it with Harbertonford, which is nearer to Kingsbridge and is on the main road. In the centre of the village turn right and then right again, aiming for the church. The pub is on the village square.

Parking: There is parking in the square and also in the lanes around the village.

Length of the walk: 4½ miles. Maps: OS Explorer OL20 South Devon; OS Landranger 202 Torbay and South Dartmoor area (GR 778586).

This is a quiet ramble through the beautiful rolling countryside so typical of the South Hams, with some lovely views and only a few fairly easy climbs to see them.

The Walk

Head back into the village from the pub, away from the church. At the crossroads go straight on. Turn right at the T-junction and then almost immediately left up a track at the bus turning area. After about 150 yards branch left down another track between a wall on the left and a high bank on the right. There is a pretty stream at the bottom of the hill on the left.

This stretch of the track can be very muddy after rain. It soon starts to climb gently with pretty hedgerows on either side, and becomes less muddy as it does so. It then descends to a farm, however, and there are more muddy patches and puddles.

Just beyond the farm, you join a lane and turn right. The lane winds up a hill, becoming a roughly surfaced track as it does so. At the top, follow it round to the right and a typical South Hams view opens up to the right and ahead, with the varied colours and textures of the fields rolling away to the purple hills and tors of Dartmoor in the distance. At the junction, go straight on. As the track curves to the left, another panorama of beautiful hills and valleys comes into view on the right.

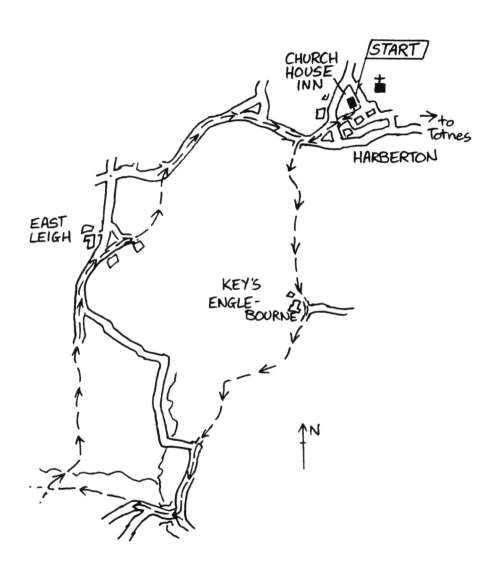

START

CHURCH
HOUSE
INN

→ to
Totnes

HARBERTON

EAST
LEIGH

KEY'S
ENGLE-
BOURNE

↑N

51

The track winds downhill, past a farm on the left, to join a lane. Go straight on, and at the junction turn right (signposted to Diptford and Avonwick). Cross a stone bridge, pass a farm, and at the fork, go right. Immediately beyond the modern house on your right, turn right through a gate (signposted 'Public footpath'). Go across the bottom of the field and through another gate. Bear slightly left across the next field to a stile in the hedge. Cross it and go *diagonally right* across the next field to a third gate, *not* to the stile on the left or the footbridge straight ahead.

Just beyond the gate you cross a stream, then go up to a gateway and along the left-hand side of the next field to yet another gate. This leads on to a track leading up a short hill between hedges. It soon levels off and the going becomes very easy. You pass an old barn on the right, and then a brand new one, with a view across the fields to the right.

The track stretches for almost ½ mile, and ends in a stile leading into a lane. Turn left and follow the lane for about 500 yards. Pass East Leigh Farm and a couple of houses on the right, and take the track on the right beyond them. After a few yards the track joins a surfaced lane, which bends sharply towards the houses on the right. As it does so, go through a gate straight ahead on to a path (signposted 'Public footpath').

Follow the path down between two walls to a gate. Go down the field beyond to another gate on the other side. Keep to the right of the next field, cross the stile at the end and head for the house you can see ahead. Cross the stile just before it and follow the drive past it to a lane, where you turn right. Cross the river Harbourne and follow the lane as it winds alongside it, with a wood climbing up the hillside on your right.

Soon the lane begins to climb steeply. At the top there is a fork. Go right, and you can see the tower of Harberton Church ahead of you. Go straight on into the village and at the bus stop turn left. Go straight across at the crossroads and back to the pub.

Haytor Vale
The Rock Inn

Haytor is one of the major landmarks of this south-eastern corner of Dartmoor; its great bulk dominates the skyline for many miles around, and can be seen from as far afield as the South Hams. Haytor Vale, as its name suggests, is a small village nestling almost in the shadow of this great outcrop of rock.

The Rock Inn is a lovely 18th century coaching inn which has been very tastefully and sympathetically decorated, with solid stone walls, exposed in places, and a number of little half-hidden corners. It is a fairly upmarket pub, offering good accommodation. The bar is decorated with plates, prints and figurines and well furnished with tables, padded chairs, settles and an old grandfather clock. Across the passageway is a lounge which doubles as a children's eating area, and behind the bar is a delightful little snug, with room for no more than about eight or ten people. The attractive beer garden is across the road.

The restaurant is another beautiful room down a passage and past some more little nooks. The bar menu, which is different for lunch and dinner, is excellent, extensive, and includes local produce.

The inn is said to be haunted by a 200-year-old ghost called Belinda. She was apparently a serving wench who was having an affair with one of the coachmen. They were caught together by the coachman's wife, who beat poor Belinda to death on the stairs.

Telephone: 01364 661305.

How to get there: From Bovey Tracey follow the signs to Haytor. Before you get to Haytor itself, turn left (signposted to Haytor Vale). Cross the cattle grid and turn left again. The pub is on the left towards the end of the village.

Parking: There is no pub car park, but you should be able to park in the road outside. At weekends in summer, when the place is crowded, you may have to park a little distance away, but you should be able to find somewhere.

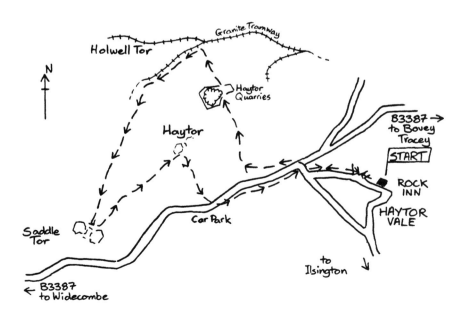

Length of the walk: 4½ miles. Maps: OS Explorer OL28 Dartmoor; OS Landranger 191 Okehampton and North Dartmoor area (GR 772772).

Haytor is a very popular place for family outings – it is an easily accessible part of the moor and children enjoy the challenge of climbing the tor. Haytor Down, the area around the tor, is full of interest both because of the remains of the granite workings to be seen here and because of the succession of breathtaking views. As it is open moorland, you can wander almost at will; the route I describe is just one of many you could choose, but it does take in some of the best viewpoints. It is an undemanding amble, unless you decide to climb Haytor, in which case you will need both agility and a head for heights!

The Walk

Turn right outside the Rock and follow the lane through the village, round to the left and up the hill. At the T-junction at the top, turn right and cross the cattle grid. Cross the road ahead on to the moorland beyond. Bear left through the gorse and bracken to join a track.

Follow the track away from the road. You will find this area – and much of the rest of the walk for that matter – a glorious mass of yellow gorse and purple heather in summer. Haytor looms to your left as you follow the track round to the left until it peters out. Aim for the end of the granite spoil heaps you can see to the right of Haytor.

When you get to these great mounds of rocks, keep to the left of them, and of the small ravine that runs alongside them, until you come to a gate on your right. This leads into the largest of the old granite quarries, now filled with water and with a few old pieces of machinery still remaining. Go round the left-hand side of the water and then curve right on the other side to a stile leading out of the quarry.

Keep to the clear path that goes straight on, with the moors stretching away before you, the jagged outline of Greator in the foreground, with Hound Tor immediately behind. Hound Tor is said to derive its name from an unfortunate incident that befell a local hunter called Bowerman centuries ago. He upset some local witches by riding through their coven, so they ambushed him in the middle of a hunt, and with their combined powers turned him into the great stone known as Bowerman's Nose near Manaton and his hounds into the rocks of Hound Tor.

Soon after leaving the quarry, the path forks; bear left. Where it forks again, bear left again and you will soon come to what looks like a railway track made of stone – which is just what it is – the granite tramway along which horses used to pull trucks filled with granite blocks. It used to run gently downhill all the way to Teigngrace, where the granite was transferred to barges and taken down to Teignmouth.

From there it was shipped to its final destinations, eventually being used in buildings such as the British Museum and London Bridge.

The tramway forks just where you join it. Take the left-hand branch and follow it along the hillside, with the stark shape of Hound Tor silhouetted against the skyline to the right and the jumble of rocks that is Holwell Tor almost straight ahead. You will notice that many of the rocks along the side of the tramway, which look as though they have been there for centuries, have grooves in their sides. These are where wedges and nails were inserted into blocks of granite and hammered home to split them into more or less even shapes.

Further on, there is a track leading off to the left to more workings. Our route goes straight on to bypass them, and straight on again at the next fork. The tramway peters out, but the path is quite clear. Just aim for the ridge of rocks you can see up ahead. There is a lovely view to the right across farms and moorland, seeming to roll on for ever. There is a gentle climb up to the rocks, and at the top more views open up – behind and ahead of you as well as to the right.

Continue along the path down the other side of the ridge, across to Saddle Tor, which you can see ahead and to your left. For the easiest route, go round to the right of the large rocks and then left on to the 'saddle'. The views from up here are the best so far, and for the first time include a panorama to the south, where you can see the sea on a clear day.

Go down left off Saddle Tor towards Haytor, still with those stunning views to left and right. You are now walking parallel to the road, but some way from it. From here you can either climb the slope ahead to Haytor or, if you are becoming blasé about views, you can skirt round to the right. I would strongly recommend the climb. It is neither very long nor very steep, and the views to the east and the south will take your breath away.

If you are feeling really energetic, you could tackle Haytor itself. Steps have been cut into the rock in places to make it a little easier, but there is still quite a lot of scrambling involved, so it is not for the old or the frail. And once you are at the top, you will need a head for heights. But if you make it, the view is spectacular.

There are a number of broad paths leading down from Haytor to the road. Take any one of them and then follow the road past the car park and Moorlands House. Turn right and retrace your route back to Haytor Vale and the pub.

13 **Hemborough Post,** near **Dartmouth**
The Sportsman's Arms

This seems a strange place to find a pub. There is no village here, not even a hamlet; Hemborough Post is no more than a crossroads. But being the only pub in the area, it does a good local trade, and it is a suitable stopping-off place along the main road from Dartmouth to Totnes.

It is quite an old pub (although no one seems to know just how old), but it has had several 'face lifts', with the result that today's building does not look a great deal like the photographs of its former self on the walls of the bar. The alterations have been very well done, resulting in a very congenial place for a drink or a bite.

There is a large, attractive front bar, with a big open fire at one end and sporting prints on the walls, and a very pleasant smaller bar leading off at the back, with a correspondingly smaller fire. Through the main bar is a lovely restaurant, very tastefully decorated. Right at the back is a family room, and to the side a garden with a super children's play area. The Sportsman's Arms prides itself on being a family pub.

The food here is excellent and ranges from simple snacks to steaks, lasagne and hearty roasts.

Telephone: 01803 712231.

How to get there: The pub is directly on the A3122 Dartmouth to Totnes road at the Hemborough Post crossroads, where the road to Dittisham branches off.

Parking: There is a large pub car park at the back, and the manager usually has no objection to customers leaving their cars there while they walk, but please ask first.

Length of the walk: 4½ miles. Maps: OS Explorer OL20 South Devon; OS Landranger 202 Torbay and South Dartmoor area (GR 831522).

Fields, woods, streams, views – this walk has them all in abundance, and an interesting little display of prehistoric life to visit along the way. And apart from a long but not too steep climb at the end, it is not too strenuous. What more could you ask?

The Walk

At the crossroads, take the road signposted to Capton and Dittisham. The views start almost immediately – if you look to the left, you can see across the farmland all the way to Dartmoor. The distinctive hump on the horizon is Haytor. After about 600 yards, you will see a public footpath sign on the left. Go through the gate and diagonally across the field beyond, still with that lovely view across a patchwork of fields to the moors on your left.

Go through the gate in the corner of the field and along the top of the next field. Keep going round, passing two gates on the right, and then down the hill. Pass a third gate and go through the fourth on to a track. Bear right and follow the track down to a lane.

Turn left into the pretty little hamlet of Capton, and after a few yards turn right (signposted 'Public bridleway'; also signposted to Dittisham Farm). After about 100 yards, a sign points to the left to Dittisham Farm, and also the Prehistoric Hill Settlement Museum.

It is worth a short stop to see the museum; it is very small, and a visit need take no more than 10 or 15 minutes. It is housed in a reconstruction of a prehistoric hut, and comprises replicas of the various weapons, food, clothing and so on that were used, together with a few artefacts from the period, and explanations of the way of life.

After your visit, continue up the track between hedges. You soon emerge into a field. Go straight up the right-hand side to a gate. Bear left after the gate and go alongside the hedge to the next gate. There is a magnificent view ahead to the Dart estuary and round Torbay. Keep to the left of the next field, as the view across to Dartmoor opens up again on the left. At the far side go through another gate on to a track.

Follow the track down through a farm to a lane and turn left. After a little over ¼ mile you will come to a T-junction. Turn left again (signposted to Cornworthy) and go down the hill to a stream. The lane winds a fair bit down here, and you soon pass a pretty stone house on your left. Just beyond it, as the lane turns sharply to the right, go left up a track signposted as unsuitable for motors.

You will pass another track leading off to the right, but just keep going straight on. Look out for pheasants in the fields on either side and wild flowers in the hedgerows alongside. You can hear the noise of the stream way down the steep slope to your right.

The track runs through a copse, mainly of chestnut, beech and oak. When you come to a stone bridge, bear left (signposted 'Public bridleway') and go through a gate and alongside the stream. Then go through another gate into the delightful Capton Wood, managed by the Woodland Trust. This is also mainly chestnut, beech and oak, with a number of other species mixed in.

The path climbs up through the wood, leaving the stream to the right. All too soon, you will come to a gate. On the other side, the wood begins to thin and you can see the stream rushing along below the bank to the right. Then there is another gate and you leave the wood altogether. Follow a broad track alongside a hedge to yet another gate and then between hedges past a farm on the right.

Go through the gate at the end to a lane and turn left. After about 250 yards there is a T-junction, with the lane going left and a track going right. Go right and cross the stream. Follow the track as it climbs gently and then descends equally gently to a lane. Turn left and brace yourself for a long climb back up to Hemborough Post. If you pause for breath on the way up, you can look back for one last view across to our old friend Haytor on the horizon. Then resume the climb, and you will come out alongside the Sportsman's Arms.

14 Hexworthy
The Forest Inn

An old coaching inn originally stood on this site, but it was destroyed by fire in 1914. The present inn is therefore relatively new, having been completed in 1916. It lies to the south of the tiny cluster of houses that is Hexworthy.

It is a fairly large pub, with an interesting layout. There are four interconnected rooms on an open-plan system, with the bar in one room and a restaurant in another. There is also a comfortable lounge area with deep armchairs and an open fire, and a fourth room for bar food. All four are light and airy, and are very tastefully decorated and furnished. At the back is a patio with tables and benches.

The staff are very welcoming, and you will find the pub a friendly, congenial place to start or finish your walk. The food is good and wide-ranging, from snacks to hot dishes such as steak and ale pie.

Telephone: 01364 631211.

How to get there: Hexworthy is just to the south of the Ashburton to Princetown road, between Dartmeet and Two Bridges. The turn-off is about ½ mile from Dartmeet and 4 miles from Two Bridges, and is clearly signposted. The pub is ¾ mile from the turn-off.

Parking: The car park is just opposite the front of the pub, and there is no objection to genuine customers leaving their cars there while they walk, provided they ask.

Length of the walk: 3 miles. Maps: OS Explorer OL28 Dartmoor; OS Landranger 191 Okehampton and North Dartmoor area (GR 655726).

This very varied walk incorporates something of everything: babbling rivers, rolling fields, open moorland and breathtaking scenery. It is all relatively easy, with only a few gentle climbs.
NOTE: *It is not a walk to do after heavy rain, however; halfway through, you have to negotiate stepping stones across the West Dart river, and although they are very easy to manage most of the time, they can become difficult when the river is in spate.*

The Walk

Go left down the road outside the pub (signposted to Princetown). As it curves left, notice the house on the left-hand side called Jolly Lane Cot, which has an interesting history. It was the last house in Devon to be built according to an ancient tradition which laid down that anyone who could enclose a piece of land, build a house on it and light a fire inside in one day between sunrise and sunset became the legal owner.

One day in 1835, when the farmers who held ancient tenants' rights to the land in the area were at Ashburton Fair, a man called Tom Satterley, with the help of local labourers, set about enclosing the land and building the house, and by the time the fair finished and the farmers returned, the fire was lit. Its appearance has changed somewhat over the years, especially with the addition of a second storey early this century and the replacement of the thatch with slates, but it is not too difficult to imagine the simple cottage that it once was.

Follow the road round the right-hand bend, cross the stream below and continue among the trees alongside it, and then alongside the rather wider West Dart river. The road continues to wind first to the left and then to the right, and crosses the river via a beautiful stone bridge. The river is now on your left, but soon curves away while the

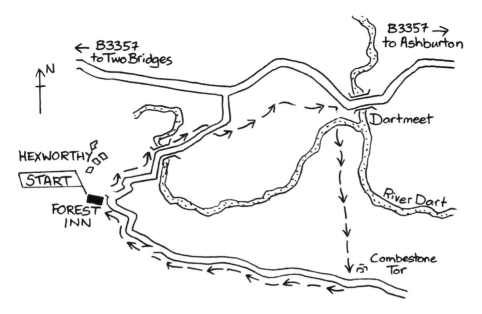

road goes straight on up a hill.

Soon after you pass the church, the road curves to the left. Turn right here up a track. After a few yards turn left (signposted 'Footpath Dartmeet') and go through a gate into a field. Cross the field, following the yellow stakes which mark the path. At the top of the rise there is a footpath sign, and you look straight ahead to Yar Tor above the popular picnic spot of Dartmeet. There are also extensive views behind you.

Continue to follow the yellow stakes (and yellow dots painted on the odd rocks) down the field to a gap in the wall on the right (signposted 'Dartmeet'). This leads you on to a path between walls, still with yellow dots painted on the rocks to show that you are on the right route. Cross a stile and continue down between two walls to a gateway on the left, marked with a yellow dot on each stone post.

Go through the gateway and follow the yellow stakes across the field beyond, down towards the house at the bottom. When you get there, go right (signposted 'Bridlepath to Combestone via stepping stones'). This takes you down to the river and the stepping stones. These are usually quite dry and easy to negotiate, but after heavy rain they can become wet or even completely covered by water. If they do happen to be covered, then it is best not to risk trying to cross and your only alternative is to return the way you came.

Once across the river, go straight on up the hill and into the trees to a gap in the wall ahead (marked with a blue waymark). Go through and follow the line of trees on your left. Go through the gap in the next wall and keep straight on, now with a wall on your left. Cross a track and carry straight on (signposted 'Bridlepath Holne road at Combestone Tor'). At the top, your view is dominated by tors on all sides: to the left, down the Dart valley, is Aish Tor; behind you is Yar Tor; to the right lie Bellever Tor, Longaford Tor and the television mast on North Hessary Tor; and ahead you can now see Combestone Tor and the rolling moorland beyond.

The track you are on crosses a cattle grid and then curves left to another (signposted 'Bridlepath Holne road at Combestone Tor'). Bear left off the track to climb up to Combestone Tor for the best views of all. You can see down into the Dart valley and beyond across moors and fields to the east and over an almost endless expanse of moorland and woods to the north and west. The tors you can now see are too numerous to list here. Suffice it to say that the panorama is quite stunning.

When you have had your fill, go right from Combestone Tor along the road. Follow it down the hill, across a bridge and cattle grid and then up the other side, still with a good view across the river to the right. At the junction, go straight on (signposted to Princetown) and down to the pub.

15 Holne
The Church House Inn

If there is such a thing as a typical Dartmoor village, then Holne is it. Unlike some places, which give the impression of being beautifully preserved but dead, Holne is a vibrant living community. It is small and compact, with traditional cottages clustered around the pub, church and shop, and a few more modern houses, which have not been allowed to spoil the character of the village, further out.

The Church House Inn, as its name suggests, is right next to the church. It is an attractive 14th century inn which was probably built as a resting place for visiting clergy and worshippers. It is a lovely old building, with beams, leaded windows and timber partitions. There are two small bars and a third room, the Kingsley Room, which serves as a lounge/family room. (The Kingsley Room is named after the author Charles Kingsley, whose father was vicar here.) Although there is no garden as such, there are benches outside and a small lawn looking out on the village. There is also a dining room, and accommodation is available.

The proprietors have been very successful in retaining the traditional atmosphere of the inn, which attracts a good mix of

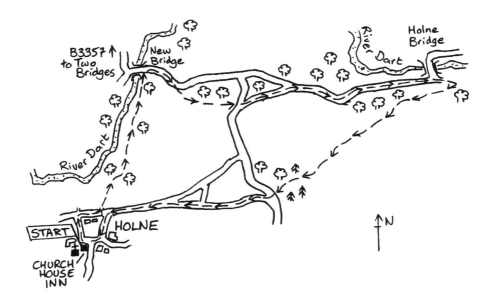

locals and visitors. The food is excellent – all home-made from fresh and where possible local and organic ingredients. There is a good selection of bar food, from ploughman's lunches and jacket potatoes to salads and fish dishes, as well as restaurant meals.

Telephone: 01364 631208.

Hot to get there: Holne is about 1½ miles from the Ashburton to Princetown road. The turn-off is about halfway between Holne Bridge and Newbridge, and is clearly signposted. At Holne, take the first turning into the village centre, and the Church House Inn is almost immediately opposite you at the bottom of the hill.

Parking: The pub has no car park. You may be able to park in the road outside, but if not, there is a free public car park just down the road that runs to the left alongside the pub and church.

Length of the walk: 4 miles. Maps: OS Explorer OL28 Dartmoor; OS Landranger 202 Torbay and South Dartmoor area (GR 706695).

There is a bit of something for everyone on this delightful route. It takes you through some lovely National Trust woodland, along a gorgeous stretch of river, across farmland, up to some good viewpoints and back down to the village.

The Walk

Turn left outside the pub and follow the road up the hill out of the village. At the top, turn right. After about 100 yards, turn left over a stile (signposted 'Public footpath'). The path goes downhill, with a hedge on the left and a fence on the right, with views ahead of you across the river Dart to the moors.

Cross the next stile into a field and go straight across to a gate with another stile alongside it. Then cross two more fields to enter Holne Woods, which are owned by the National Trust.

The path curves down through the woods, with the river Dart way below it on the left. At the bottom it joins a track (signposted 'Footpath Newbridge'), which takes you alongside the river as it tumbles and burbles over the rocks on the left. The effects of the light filtering through the trees and playing on the water along here on a sunny day can be quite beautiful.

When the track curves to the right, bear left on to a path (signposted 'Footpath'). You can still hear the river on your left, although it is hidden by the trees along here. You finally leave Holne Woods through a kissing-gate which leads on to the road. On the left just outside the gate is Newbridge, a lovely old stone packhorse bridge which has not actually been 'new' since the 15th century.

Our route goes to the right outside the gate, to follow the road a short distance up the hill. Just beyond the house called Rivermead, turn right across a stile and then left to skirt the field on the other side. Go through the gap in the hedge to the next field, climbing all the time, with Kinghurst Down Wood on your left. If you stop to catch your breath on the way up, look back the way you have come for an attractive view across the valley to the fields and woods beyond.

There is a stile at the end of the field, followed by a short path which takes you to a road. Turn left here, and then after 100 yards or so fork right (signposted to Ashburton). At the main road, turn right and follow the road down to Holne Bridge, another 15th century packhorse bridge – a distance of about ½ mile.

Where the road turns left to cross the bridge, go straight on up a drive (signposted to Holne Park). After about 50 yards turn sharp right up a track (signposted 'Public footpath Gallant le Bower'). After another 50 yards or so, turn left up another track, following the path sign, and a few yards further on, turn sharp right, again following the footpath sign.

At a fork, go left, still following the footpath sign. Towards the top of the hill, a sign points to the left across a stile. Go over the stile and turn right up a track along the outside of the wood.

When the boundary of the wood turns off to the right, follow the line of trees which goes straight on. Cross a stile into the next field, still with the line of trees on your left. There is a good view across to the right. Cross the stile at the end of the field to enter a short stretch of woodland (signposted 'Public footpath').

After about 100 yards the path joins a track. Follow this track to the right, until it emerges at a crossroads. Take the road almost immediately opposite you, signposted to Holne. As you go down the hill, you will occasionally catch glimpses of the superb view to the right, across the river and fields to a number of tors beyond. At the T-junction, turn left (signposted to Holne again). After about ¼ mile, turn left to go into the village and back to the pub.

16 Hope Cove
The Hope and Anchor Inn

Hope Cove is in two parts – Outer Hope and Inner Hope. The Hope and Anchor is in Outer Hope, a delightful old fishing village with narrow streets and quaint old houses.

The inn is about 300 years old. It is a pleasant building of stone and brick comprising the plain but comfortable Family Bar, with games etc, the delightful Yacht Lounge, with an open fire, and the separate Boathouse Restaurant. The best place to be on a sunny summer's day, however, is sitting at the tables outside on the forecourt, watching the activity and enjoying the views out to sea.

The range of food is impressive, from snacks to main meals and includes a variety of fish dishes.

Telephone: 01548 561294.

How to get there: Hope Cove is in Bigbury Bay, just below the headland called Bolt Tail. To get there, follow the A381 Kingsbridge to Salcombe road. About halfway to Salcombe there is a turn-off to the right, signposted to Hope Cove. Follow it through Galmpton, and when you reach Hope Cove follow the signs for Outer Hope. The pub is on the left just beyond the car park.

Parking: There is no pub car park, but between October and March you can park just up the road. The only parking during the summer months, however, is in the pay and display car park on the left just before you reach the old part of the village.

Length of the walk: 4¾ miles. Maps: OS Explorer OL20 South Devon; OS Landranger 202 Torbay and South Dartmoor area (GR 676401).

For delightful coastal walking with spectacular views but without the steep climbs that so often go with them, this route takes a lot of beating.

The Walk

Follow the road which leads down past the Hope and Anchor into the village. Keep to the same road as it runs above the beach, and when it ends follow the path ahead. Steps lead up to the left, and the path runs between a fence on the left and a hedge on the right, over which you can look out to the cove and the cliffs beyond.

At the top you join the road which links Outer Hope to Inner Hope. Turn right (signposted 'Coast Path') and at the T-junction right again (signposted 'Coast Path Bolt Tail'). Just beyond the slipway at the bottom of the hill, turn right up some steps (signposted 'Coast Path Bolt Head, Salcombe'). Go through the kissing-gate and into some woodland. This marks the start of the National Trust property which stretches all the way to Bolt Head.

Climb up to the open country. The going is not too steep, and when you emerge from the woodland, you can see all the way back along the coast. Soon the path forks. Go right to reach Bolt Tail. There is an interesting Iron Age earthwork here; make sure that you keep to the path to avoid damage to the embankment. At Bolt Tail the true grandeur of this part of the coastline becomes apparent as you look westwards. On a clear day you can see the cliffs, bays and beaches stretching away into the distance – as far as Rame Head, in Cornwall.

The path turns left to follow the line of the cliffs. After about ½ mile you come to a gate and a stile leading to a stretch of open downland between the cliffs and a field (signposted 'Coast Path'). Look to the left for another superb view across Hope Cove and the farmland beyond

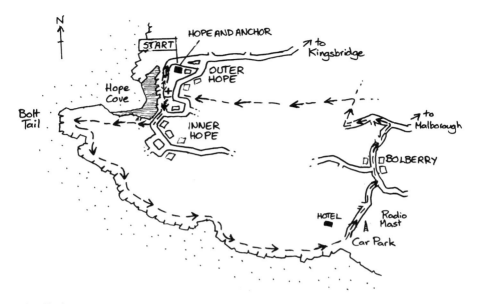

it all the way to Dartmoor. After another mile or so, you will cross another stile on to Bolberry Down.

Follow the path along the edge of the down for a while, with a mass of wild flowers tumbling away to your right, down to the sea. You will soon come to a tarred path leading to the left, towards a mast. Follow it until it joins the drive leading to the Port Light Hotel. Turn right here, and at the lane at the end, turn left. Cross the cattle grid and follow the lane past the mast and the group of houses on the right. There are more views from here across to Dartmoor.

At the bottom of the hill turn left. Where the road curves left to Hope Cove a few yards further on, go straight on up a narrow lane between banks. Follow the lane round a gorgeous stone and thatch cottage and up a steep hill until you come to the Broadmoor crossroads. Turn sharp left here down a track (signposted 'Footpath to Hope Cove, Galmpton'), which leads to the gate of Higher Barton.

Turn right immediately before the gate (signposted 'Footpath Hope Cove, Galmpton') and follow the overgrown path to a stile. Cross the field beyond to another stile. Keep to the right of the next field and go through the gate at the top. Turn immediately left. From here you can see the coastline stretching away ahead of you, with farmland across to the right, rolling away to the moors.

This view stays with you as you cross five fields, keeping to the top (the left) of each. At the end of the last field, take the track which bears left and follow it down to a gate. Go through and follow the lane down to the road at Inner Hope. Cross the road and go down the steps and path alongside the church. At the bottom turn right (signposted 'Coast Path') on to the path you took from Outer Hope and follow it back to the village and the pub.

17 Ivybridge
The Exchange

As you would expect from a town of its size, Ivybridge has several good pubs. I like the Exchange because it is one of the most attractive and welcoming, and because its position makes it an ideal starting point for exploring this part of Dartmoor.

It is quite a large pub, comprising one L-shaped room divided into separate but interconnected sections and alcoves by arched stone walls and panelled partitions. One section is the main bar, another the lounge, a third has a pool table, and a fourth is an eating area. It is very tastefully decorated, furnished and carpeted.

Food ranges from bar snacks, including ploughman's and sandwiches, to main meals such as lasagne and various tempting pies.

Telephone: 01752 896677.

How to get there: Follow the signs from the A38 into Ivybridge, then follow the signs for the town centre car park. The Exchange is in Exeter Road, at the start of the pedestrianised area.

Parking: The pub has no car park. Park in the main town centre car park and walk through to Exeter Road.

Length of the walk: 5½ miles. Maps: OS Explorer OL28 Dartmoor or OL20 South Devon; OS Landranger 202 Torbay and South Dartmoor area (GR 635563).

This southern part of Dartmoor is not quite as wild and bleak as the more northerly section, but it has a magnificent landscape nevertheless, and the walking is superb. The route I have chosen includes some of the most attractive moorland in the area, together with some lovely farmland and a few quiet and attractive lanes. There is just one fairly steep climb, but even that can be avoided if you wish – though at the expense of some stunning views.

The Walk

Turn right from the pub into Exeter Road, cross the bridge and turn left into Harford Road. You follow the river Erme for a while and then the road winds to the right, passing a paper mill on the left and then Ivybridge Community College on the right. It climbs out of town and at the crossroads at the top you cross over into a lane (signposted to Harford).

Cross the railway line and follow the lane for a short distance until you come to Stowford Farm on your left. Turn right up a track opposite the farm (signposted 'Public bridlepath to the moor'). Do not go through either of the gates ahead of you, but follow the track to the left. It takes you through a gate and climbs quite steeply between two walls, winding to the right and then to the left. There is then a gentler climb to a gate, beyond which is the moor.

Because it is open moorland, there are few clearly marked paths in this area. But in this kind of terrain it is your direction and the landmarks you aim for that are important rather than the precise route you choose for getting there.

If you look to your right as you come through the gate, you will see Western Beacon, while Butterdon Hill is half-right ahead of you. It is the latter you should be aiming for, so bear slightly right from the gate. The going is very easy over the soft grass here, and there is an incredible stillness all around. A lovely view of a patchwork of fields opens up behind you as you go, and to the left you can see Shell Top and the rather ugly china clay works of Lee Moor in the distance.

About ½ mile from the gate you come to a track. Cross over it for

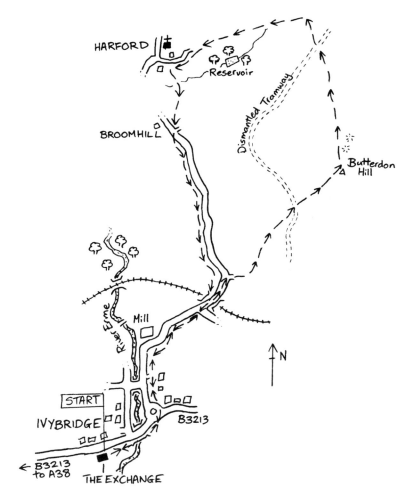

the moderately steep climb up Butterdon Hill, and the breathtaking views from the top. You can see for miles in almost every direction, with only Western Beacon to the south and Ugborough Beacon to the east to spoil the 360-degree panorama. The moors seem to stretch endlessly to the north and the west, while to the south-east and the south-west the variegated farmland rolls away into the distance.

If you do not want to climb the hill, then turn left at the track and follow it as it skirts Weatherdon Hill, to rejoin our route further north.

From the top of Butterdon Hill, turn half-left, heading due north.

Keep the distinctive granite outcrop of Hangershell Rock on your left. As you go, you will lose the views to the east and south, but the ones to the north and west stay with you. Just beyond Hangershell Rock, you pass a cairn on the right, and then come to a stone row. It is not a particularly good example of the phenomenon – there are many others on the moor that are better preserved – but the remnants stretch for quite a long way, and it is interesting to speculate on its purpose.

Follow the stones across a track, which is where those who decided not to climb Butterdon Hill rejoin the route. Bear left. As before, there is no clear path, but aim to the right of the patch of loose boulders clearly visible down below. As you traverse the boulder field, you will see a clump of trees surrounding a reservoir to the left. Aim for a point about 200 yards to the right of those trees. As you come over the rise, you get a good view of mixed moorland and fields, but still with the china clay works in the distance.

Immediately ahead you will see a wall. If you are lucky, and your aim has been particularly accurate, you should reach it just where a gate leads into a lane. If you cannot see a gate but there is a track running just in front of the wall, then you are too far to the left, so turn right and follow the track until it turns into the gate. If there is no track, just the wall, then you are too far to the right, so you should turn left and follow the wall until you come to the track and the gate.

Go through the gate and follow the lane down to Harford. Shortly before you reach the T-junction, turn left up a drive (signposted 'Public footpath to road near Broomhill'). After about 100 yards, go left through a gate into a field (signposted 'Public footpath'). Turn right and skirt round the edge of the field to cross a delightful stream. Go through a gate on the other side and climb between some boulders to a kissing-gate just next to the gate of a house.

Cross the field beyond (signposted 'Footpath'), and go through the gap in the wall at the top and straight across to a kissing-gate, with a yellow waymark on the wall alongside. Do not follow the more obvious track to the large gate on the right. Cross the next field diagonally to a gate and keep to the left of the next one. At the end, cross a stone stile to join a lane and turn left.

This lane meanders gently and very pleasantly back to Ivybridge, past farms and through woodland. Towards the end, a lovely view opens up ahead. At the crossroads, go straight across to the road you came up at the start and follow it as it winds down into the town. Turn right at the bottom to return to the Exchange.

18 Kingston
The Dolphin Inn

Kingston is a small village not far from the coast. Although there has been a fair amount of development around the edges, the heart of the village retains its charm, with traditional thatched cottages, a beautiful old church, and of course the pub.

The Dolphin is a 16th century inn with thick stone walls and shuttered windows. Inside it has low beamed ceilings and has been very tastefully decorated. There is an interesting collection of mugs of all kinds, and a fascinating array of foreign bank notes pinned to the beams. The interior is divided into three areas, all done out in the same style and furnished with benches and tables.

There is an extensive menu, ranging from bar snacks to main meals, and a wide variety of daily specials. Fish dishes predominate in the summer with game taking up the baton in the winter.

Across the lane there is a large garden, with swings for children, and a very pleasant family room.

Telephone: 01548 810314.

How to get there: Kingston is just off the B3392 Modbury to Bigbury-on-Sea road and is clearly signposted. When you reach the outskirts of the village, you will see signs pointing to the inn.

Parking: The inn has a large car park. There is no restriction on parking in the village, but the roads are rather narrow, so it may not be easy to find somewhere suitable. The landlord of the Dolphin is happy for customers to leave their cars in his car park while they walk, as long as they ask permission first.

Length of the walk: 5½ miles. Maps: OS Explorer OL20 South Devon; OS Landranger 202 Torbay and South Dartmoor area (GR 635478).

This lovely walk combines woodland, beaches and spectacular clifftop views along the South-West Coast Path. There are some very steep ascents along the cliffs, but if you can make it, the rewards are well worth the effort. Trousers rather than shorts are recommended, as one stretch can be overgrown.

The Walk

Turn right outside the pub and right again at the T-junction. Follow the road up a hill out of the village. After about 200 yards, turn left into a long straight lane. As you walk along it, look out for pheasants in the fields on either side. The lane itself is very pretty in summer, with a variety of hedgerow flowers in bloom.

At the end of the lane, follow the 'Public bridleway' sign down a track to the right. Go through the gate at the end, along the edge of a field and down a very steep hill. At the bottom, turn right (signposted 'Permissive footpath Westcombe Beach'). Cross a stile, go through a short stretch of beautiful cool woodland and cross the footbridge at the end. The path now takes you between a stream and a field down towards Westcombe Beach, with a mass of wild flowers all around. Unfortunately there are also a lot of nettles and brambles along this section, so it is advisable to wear trousers.

Just before you get to Westcombe Beach, you cross a stile. Turn right here. The path skirts the delightful beach, but it is very easy to make your way down to the sand if you want to. If not, go through a gate and climb the very steep hill in front of you. It seems to go on for ever, but you *will* get to the top eventually, and when you do, the views are stunning. Look back the way you have come, and you can

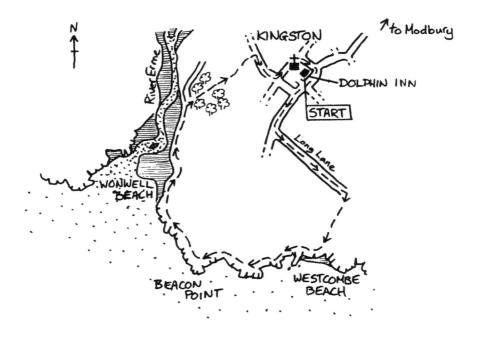

see all the way along the coast to Burgh Island, Bolt Tail, and on a clear day Prawle Point. Looking inland, it is as if the whole of the South Hams are laid out before you in a patchwork of fields and colour.

From here the path goes up and down several times, but none of the climbs is as steep as the first one.

You eventually go round Beacon Point and yet another magnificent panorama opens up before you. You can see along the coast ahead all the way to Stoke Point, and then inland across fields and farms – on a clear day as far as Dartmoor. You then round Fernycombe Point and come to the extensive sands of the Erme estuary. Cross a stile at the bottom of the field and skirt a field as the path follows the estuary through a patch of scrub. At the end, cross another stile and descend to Wonwell Beach. This is a lovely beach – golden sands stretching all the way across the estuary at low tide – and it is an ideal place to take a break and cool your feet after your exertions. The most strenuous part of the walk is behind you; all that is left is a comparatively gentle stroll back to the village.

Cross the stream immediately in front of you as you come down from the path and take the path on the other side, leading up on to the bank above. Continue up the estuary, through a tunnel of trees, and enter a wood. After about 200 yards you leave it again, via some steps down to a road. Turn right. A few yards up the road, a path leads off to the right, back into the wood (signposted to Kingston).

The path meanders through this lovely wood, climbing all the time. At the top there is a stile into a field. The path runs along the top of the field, at the end of which you cross another stile into another field. There are more beautiful views along this stretch, mainly of fields and rolling countryside.

At the end of this field, the path goes to the right of the gate, across a stile – it is not always easy to find, as it is a bit overgrown. After a few yards there is another stile. Go diagonally across the next field, and on the far side go round to the left, keeping the hedge on your right. Cross a stile and go on to the next gateway, where there is another stile leading into a lane.

Turn right and follow the lane back to Kingston. At the crossroads, turn left and then right past the church to the Dolphin. You can also go through the churchyard and visit the beautiful old church, with its somewhat unusual tower. It looks as though the taller, narrower section, with the clock on it, has been stuck on to the corner of the main tower. As a result, the clock is off-centre, giving the whole structure a lopsided appearance.

20 Woolston Green
The Live and Let Live Inn

Woolston Green is a delightful little place, with a pretty, tree-shaded green. Although the pub sign shows a fox and a badger living in harmony, the name 'Live and Let Live' is said to derive from the inn's position right next to the Methodist chapel, and the idea that churchgoers and topers should tolerate each other. It is about 200 years old, and was once a private house; indeed, it still has that appearance. Inside, it is a cosy little place, with a very friendly welcome. There is just the one bar, with a family room, behind it.

In addition to the rooms inside, there are tables in the sunny front garden and a delightfully shaded beer garden in an orchard across the road.

Telephone: 01803 762663.

How to get there: Turn off the A38 Exeter to Plymouth road at Pear Tree Cross (the second Ashburton exit coming from the Exeter direction, the first coming from Plymouth) and follow the signs to Landscove. Go straight through and on to Woolston Green. The pub is on the left at the end of the village, with the car park on the right.

Parking: The car park is opposite the pub. Parking in the road is difficult, but the proprietors have no objection to customers leaving their cars in the pub car park while walking.

Length of the walk: 2½ miles. Maps: OS Explorer OL28 Dartmoor (start and finish); OS Explorer 110 Torquay and Dawlish (middle section); OS Landranger 202 Torbay and South Dartmoor area (GR 779661).

If you want a delightful, gentle ramble that gives you a feel for the glorious rolling countryside of this relatively empty area of South Devon, then this is the route for you. It is mainly farmland, with a few pretty and deserted lanes, and one particularly good view across to Dartmoor.

The Walk
The path leads off from the orchard beer garden across the road from the pub itself, with a public footpath sign to show you the way. Cross the stile and keep to the right-hand side of the field on the other side to reach another stile. A small, recently planted, stretch of woodland follows, then yet another stile. Cross the next field, under the electricity cables to a gate on to the road at the Barkingdon Business Park. The going is easy, and the surrounding area is typical of South Devon – mixed farming giving the scene a delightful variety of colours and textures. Note the distinctive red soil in the ploughed fields

Turn right and immediately left at the drive of the business park. On the corner, you will find a stile on the right, with yellow waymarks. Cross it and go left along the field beyond to a gate. Cross a track to another gate. Turn right in the field beyond and follow the hedge along the top, then left to a gateway about a third of the way down.

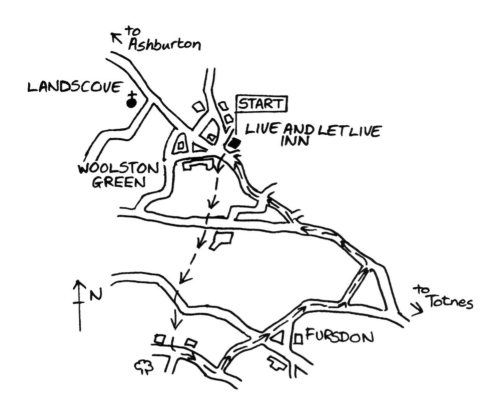

Cross the next field to another gate which you can see quite clearly on the other side. This leads into a pretty little orchard – an absolute picture when the blossom is out. Cross this to a gate which leads into a lane. Turn left.

Turn right through the *second* gate you come to. Keep to the right of the field to reach a stile and a footbridge. Cross the next field to a gap in the fence, and then make your way straight across the next field to a gate some way to the left of the house you can see in front of you. This leads on to a short track which takes you to another gate and into a lane.

Turn left down the lane, and at the bottom, just after it crosses a stream, turn left up a track between a hedge and a wood (signposted 'Public bridleway'). This is a pretty stretch, with a variety of flowers on either side. It leads up to a road. Cross the road to another short track, which joins another road. Turn left here and follow the road up the hill. At the top there is an extensive view of the farms and woodland rolling away to Dartmoor – you can clearly see the distinctive shape of Haytor on the horizon, several miles away. Bear left with the road, passing under the electricity cables again, and follow it for almost a mile back to the village and the pub.

21 Loddiswell
The Loddiswell Inn

This attractive little village sits high above the river Avon in the heart of the glorious South Hams. A short distance south of the village is Sorley Tunnel Adventure Farm.

Right in the middle of the village is the Loddiswell Inn, and old coaching inn dating back to 1800. Prisoners used to be kept overnight here before being transferred to a proper prison – which was not as pleasant an experience as it may sound, as they were kept locked away behind stout wooden doors, well away from the temptations of the flesh!

It is a delightful pub, with low beams and a mixture of stone, brick and panelled walls. There is a pleasant eating area up some steps at the end of the bar, and a terrace at the front where you can enjoy the sun.

The food is very good, ranging from sandwiches to fresh fish and meat dishes. The place is especially renowned locally for its Sunday roasts.

Telephone: 01548 550308.

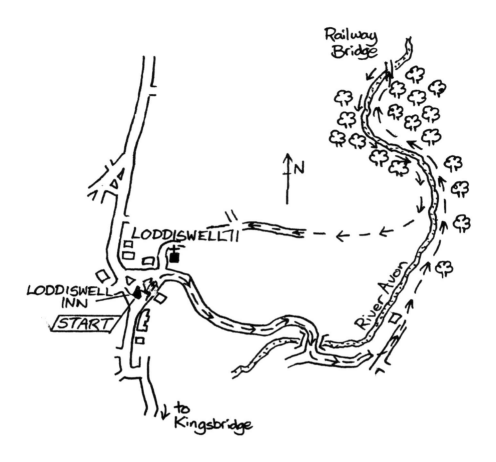

How to get there: The village is north-west of Kingsbridge, about 2¾ miles from the A381 as it bypasses the town. It is clearly signposted. The Loddiswell Inn is in the middle of the village, so if you just follow the road as it twists and winds, you are bound to find it. It can also be approached from the north-west by leaving the A38 at Wrangaton Cross, following the A3121 for about a mile before turning left at Kitterford Cross, and then following the signs to Loddiswell.

Parking: The pub has no parking, but there is a free public car park just 100 yards up the road, and it is clearly signposted.

Length of the walk: 3 miles. Maps: OS Explorer OL20 South Devon; OS Landranger 202 Torbay and South Dartmoor area (GR 720485).

Cool woods to wander through, a tumbling river to picnic by, still pools, green lanes ... this walk has them all – plus a disused railway called the Primrose Line.

The Walk

The route starts at Well Street, the lane which runs down the hill opposite the inn. Follow it down as it curves to the right and then leaves the village. Once out in the country, it begins to descend steeply until, just over ¼ mile from the pub, you come to Avon Mill Garden Centre on your left. Cross the bridge beyond the garden centre and turn left at the T-junction.

The road curves right under an old railway bridge, and then left. Soon you come to the old Loddiswell Station, now a private house. Leave the road here, taking the path just to the right of the house (signposted 'Public footpath'). This takes you into Woodleigh Wood, a Woodland Trust property. Initially the path is hemmed in by a fence on the left and an embankment. You can hear the river on your left, but you have to wait a while before it comes into sight through the trees.

The disused railway's name, the Primrose Line, comes from the mass of primroses along the route, and they are still there, providing a carpet of yellow in the spring. Follow the line of the river, with the wood climbing steeply up the hill to the right. It is a gorgeous wood, full of birds, with little rivulets tumbling down the hillside and flowing across the path, wild flowers all around and the gurgling of the river ever present in the background. In addition to the path you are on, there are others leading off to the right which you can explore. As long as you do not stray too far from the line of the river, you are unlikely to get lost.

After a while, you will find the railway track alongside you on the left, and soon you will be able to cross it and go down to the riverbank. There are several delightful spots along here, ideal for a rest or a picnic, with the river tumbling and chattering by in front of you. The path meanders through the trees until, about ¾ mile from the start of the wood, you pass a weir.

Above the weir, the river curves to the right and its character changes. It flows much more smoothly, and therefore quietly, than below the weir, with some still, deep pools. The silence in the wood is now broken only by birdsong. The path climbs to the right to join the track of the railway. There are other paths off to the right which you can explore if you wish, but our route goes left to follow the track across a bridge.

Immediately after the bridge, turn down a path to the left on to the other riverbank. At the path junction go straight on. Cross a footbridge and then a stile into a field. At the end, cross another stile to re-enter the wood. After a while you turn left to cross a dried leat, then turn right again to continue along the river.

The path eventually leaves the river and follows a small stream uphill, first to the right of it, then to the left. You eventually go through a gate onto a lane. Follow it up the hill and at the crossroads go straight on (signposted to Loddiswell and Kingsbridge). Follow the lane into Loddiswell and past the church. You will find both the car park and the pub on your right in the centre of the village.

Lustleigh
The Cleave

(22)

Lustleigh is one of the most attractive villages in Devon. The inn and the old cottages cluster round the 13th century church in traditional fashion, giving it a timeless beauty which is hard to match.

'Cleave' means valley, and the pub is named after Lustleigh Cleave, a beautifully wooded stretch of the Bovey valley to the west of the village, through which this walk passes.

It is a lovely 15th century thatched inn in the heart of the village, with a small, cosy bar and a dining-room at the front, and a family room and a larger bar, which is used mainly for overflow purposes, at the back. There is a vast inglenook fireplace in the front bar, and in the dining-room the huge granite walls have been exposed. The family room is a comfortable, welcoming room. The garden is gorgeous, and looks out on the old church and the village green.

There is a good selection of food, ranging from imaginative and sustaining bar meals to a full restaurant menu, with separate selections for lunch and dinner.

Telephone: 01647 277223.

How to get there: The village is just to the west of the A382 Bovey Tracey to Moretonhampstead road, about 4 miles from Bovey Tracey, and is signposted from the main road. The Cleave is opposite the church in the centre of the village.

Parking: The pub car park is very small and is reserved for those actually visiting the pub, but parking can be found on the road.

Length of the walk: 5 miles. Maps: OS Explorer OL28 Dartmoor; OS Landranger 191 Okehampton and North Dartmoor area (GR 785813).

After some fairly steep climbing, this beautifully varied walk takes you along the bracken- and gorse-covered top of Lustleigh Cleave, with magnificent views in all directions, and then brings you back along the densely wooded slopes below.

The Walk

Go right from the pub and up the hill, with the church on your left. Follow the road round to the right and at the war memorial, turn left. As the road curves to the right, bear left up a track marked

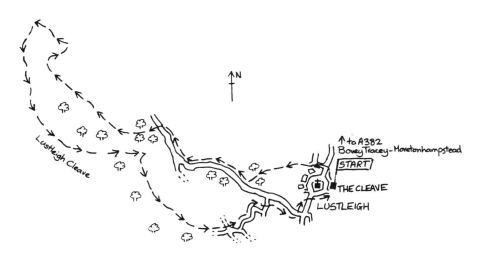

'Private drive'. Just before the gate at the end there is a path leading off to the right. Follow it through a kissing-gate into a field. Bear left along the hedge to another gate and into a wood. Go straight on to cross a small stream, follow the track up to a lane and turn right.

The lane curves to the left and climbs steeply into a wood. It winds past a farm and continues to climb to a T-junction. Turn right here and follow the lane for about 250 yards until you find a path leading off to the left (signposted 'Public bridlepath Cleave, for Water, Foxworthy, Hunter's Tor').

This path takes you between high banks and through a gate into another wood. Carry straight on up (signposted 'Public bridlepath Hunter's Tor & road near Barnecourt'). The path climbs steeply through the beautiful wood, past enormous outcrops of rock, to emerge at the top near Sharpitor.

Here it curves to the right, following the line of a wall. You can pause here, happy in the knowledge that the worst of the climbing is now over, and appreciate the superb view across to the left over Lustleigh Cleave to Hound Tor, Manaton and beyond. You are now in open country, walking mainly through bracken, and the view to the left stays with you for about ¾ mile, though obscured from time to time by stunted oaks.

Soon you will find the bracken interspersed in summer with the brilliant yellow of gorse and then replaced by grass as you emerge to some quite exceptional views through 360 degrees: there is the same view across the Cleave to the left; ahead lie North Bovey, Moreton-hampstead and the high moor; to the right are the gentler contours of farms and woods; and behind you can see all the way to the sea on a clear day.

Immediately ahead of you is Hunter's Tor, which you can climb to enhance the view if you wish. The path, however, passes through the gate just to the right of the tor (signposted simply 'Path'), and goes down the hill alongside the wall on the right. At the fence at the bottom turn left along a track (again signposted 'Path'), through two gates ('Path' again) and down to the farm below.

Go through another gate and straight across the farmyard to a concrete track leading down to the left. As the track curves right, turn left through a gate (signposted 'Foxworthy Bridge'). This path can be rather muddy at the start in wet weather, but it improves lower down. It winds down between hedges and walls to the valley below, coming out at a track. Turn right past some thatched holiday cottages, and after a few yards turn left (signposted 'Public bridlepath Hammerslake & for footpath Horsham').

Follow the track to a gate and bear right. At the fork, turn left (signposted 'Public bridlepath') and go through a gate into the wood.

After a few yards turn left again (signposted 'Path'). You can hear the river chattering along to your right as you meander through the beautiful, lush green woodland. Where the path forks, go left (waymarked in blue and signposted 'Public bridlepath Hammerslake for Lustleigh').

Soon the sound of the river becomes more distant as you climb gently up the side of the valley. Near the top of the wood, the path goes right and levels off. You eventually come to a T-junction. Turn right (signposted 'Manaton via Water') and follow a steep path down to a fork. Go left (signposted 'Lustleigh via Pethybridge'). As you go along this stretch, notice how the character of the woodland changes, as silver birch replaces oak as the predominant species, only for the oaks to take over again further on.

At the junction, go straight on (signposted 'Bridlepath Lustleigh'), and when you come to a gate, go left up the hill rather than going through the gate. Pass through the gate at the top, and up a path between hedges to join a farm track. Go straight on, following the track until it joins a lane. Turn right here, and after about 50 yards left into Pethybridge.

You will pass a beautiful thatched house on your right, and immediately afterwards you should turn right down a lane marked as unsuitable for wide vehicles. This takes you down a steep hill and curves sharply, first to the right and then to the left. At the bottom, turn right, and at the next T-junction go left. This road will take you into the centre of the village. Just before the church, turn right to return to the pub.

23 Marldon
The Church House Inn

At first sight, Marldon appears to be little more than a suburb of nearby Paignton, with streets of modern housing – not unattractive, but definitely suburban. However, at the extreme northern end of the village you will find the old part – a narrow road flanked by traditional cottages, the pretty church and the Church House Inn.

It is an attractive 15th century building, with a large bar divided into a lounge and a bar area, and a restaurant which used to be the village bakery – a feature of the room is the old ovens, which have been retained. There is a wood-burning stove in the bar and an open fire in the restaurant. There are large gardens at the back, next to the car park.

The menu is varied and interesting, ranging from snacks to main courses using local produce extensively.

Telephone: 01803 558279.

How to get there: Marldon lies just to the west of the A380 Torbay Ring Road. Leave the ring road at the Preston Downs roundabout, following the Marldon sign. Cross the next roundabout into Five Lanes Road. After 150 yards or so, turn right into Marldon Cross Hill. After about ¼ mile this road narrows and begins to twist and turn. Continue through the old part of the village and you will find the pub at the end, just beyond the church on the left.

Parking There is a large pub car park, and a free public car park across the road. The landlord has no objection to customers leaving their cars at the pub while walking.

Length of the walk: 5 miles. Maps: OS Explorer 110 Torquay and Dawlish; OS Landranger 202 Torbay and South Dartmoor area (GR 866636).

Berry Pomeroy Castle is an interesting, and supposedly haunted, ruin. This delightful walk takes you there and back through beautiful rolling farmland and along quiet country lanes.

The Walk

Turn right outside the pub and go through the attractive churchyard to a track on the other side. Turn right and go up the hill, where the track meets the Ipplepen road. Turn right again here. After 100 yards

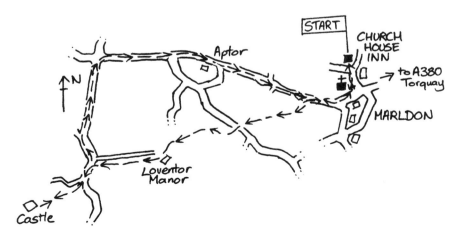

or so you will see a public footpath sign on the left. Go through the gate and follow the path that runs between a house on the left and a hedge on the right.

Cross the fence at the end into a field. Go down the side of this field to a stile, after which the path passes between a fence and a hedge and crosses a track into some woodland. At the end of the woodland you will find some steps over a wall into the next field. To the left is a pleasant view across the fields.

At the end of this field there is a kissing-gate. Go through it and follow the steep, narrow path which leads down through another small clump of trees to the road. Turn right here, and then immediately left to cross a stile (signposted 'Path'). This path bears left around a field, with extensive views across to the right, stretching right away to the moors. In the far corner, there is a stile. Cross it and turn left to follow the line of the hedge, still enjoying the views across to Dartmoor on the right.

At the end, follow the fence to the right until you come to another stile, which takes you into another field. Keep to the left down here to reach a gate leading on to a track. Turn left and follow the track as it curves round to the right and up a slight slope. Where it meets a lane, turn left. With woods on the left and a farm on the right, this stretch is full of wildlife, so keep your eyes open.

At the T-junction, turn left. You can just see the ruins of Berry Pomeroy Castle above you on the right. Take the first turning right into a lane marked with a 'no through road' sign. After about 50 yards you will see a kissing-gate on your left with a public footpath sign. Turn off here and follow the pretty path up through the woods to the castle. There is a little tearoom near the castle gate if you need refreshment, and toilets behind it.

Berry Pomeroy Castle is an English Heritage property. The ruins of the medieval castle and the 16th century mansion within it perch on the very edge of the hillside, overlooking the beautiful valley of Gatcombe Brook. It is reputedly the most haunted castle in Devon, and there are several legends and stories associated with it. The most famous concerns two sisters, Eleanor and Margaret Pomeroy, who were both in love with the same man. Eleanor, who was mistress of the castle, imprisoned her sister in one of the dungeons, where she finally died. Now her beautiful ghost is said to walk the ramparts from time to time, and beckons to anyone who sees her to join her in the dungeon.

There is another delightful piece of folklore, this time connected with the large and very old tree which stands at the top of the path you have just come up. This is called the wishing tree, and it is said that if you walk around it three times backwards and wish, your wish will come true.

To return to Marldon, follow the footpath back down through the woods to the lane at the bottom. Turn right and then left at the road. But instead of turning right to follow the lane down which you came on the outward journey, keep to the road, following it round to the left and up the hill. There are two pretty thatched cottages on your left; after the second one turn right up a lane and follow it for about ½ mile to a junction. Turn right here (signposted to Marldon, Paignton and Torquay).

After another ½ mile or so, as the road curves to the right, bear left up a track (signposted 'Marldon Lane'). This takes you up to Aptor Farm; at the track junction go straight on to join a lane. Go straight on again until the lane meets the Marldon to Ipplepen road. Turn right here and follow the road back to Marldon. Just after you enter the village, turn left down the track you came up at the beginning of the walk and through the churchyard back to the pub.

near Postbridge
The Warren House Inn

Standing high and isolated on the open moor between Postbridge and Moretonhampstead, the Warren House looks as bleak as the moorland which surrounds it on all sides. One wonders why there should be an inn in such a desolate spot, miles away from human habitation. The reason lies in the tin-workings which dot the surrounding area. This was a tin-miner's pub, although the name derives from another trade – that of the warreners, the men who 'farmed' the rabbits with which this part of the moor abounds.

Despite its uninviting exterior, the inside of this pub is snug and welcoming, with a warm atmosphere. It was built on its present site in 1845, having originally stood on the other side of the road. There are two fires in the single bar, one of which is never allowed to go out – tradition has it that this is to keep the Devil away.

There is a delightful story associated with this inn. It tells of a traveller who called there on a bitter winter's night and asked for shelter. When he was shown to his room, he found a large chest in the corner, and in a moment of idle curiosity decided to see what was inside. Imagine his horror when he found a corpse! He ran downstairs yelling 'Murder! Murder!' only to be met by the landlady, who calmly said, 'Don't fret yourself, me lover. It's only feyther.' The old man had apparently died shortly before, but because of the bad weather they had not been able to bury him. So they had salted him and stored him in the chest until the weather broke!

The pub retains its traditional atmosphere, with a bare floor, blackened beams and old wooden benches and settles. It is popular with walkers, and there are usually one or two to be found drying out before its fire on a wet day. A range of delicious home-made bar snacks, including sandwiches and ploughman's lunches, is served at lunchtime and in the evening, with main meals also available in the evening. There is a children's room off the bar, as well as benches and tables on the moorland across the road.

Telephone: 01822 880208.

How to get there: The inn is on the B3212 Postbridge to Moretonhampstead road about 3½ miles north-east of Postbridge.

Parking: The inn has no car park, but you can park on the verge of the road. Alternatively, there is a small parking area about 200 yards up the road towards Moretonhampstead.

Length of the walk: 3¾ miles. Maps: OS Explorer OL28 Dartmoor; OS Landranger 191 Okehampton and North Dartmoor area (GR 674809).

This is a walk which offers a bit of everything – history, archaeology, legend and wild open moorland, with some spectacular views thrown in for good measure. There is some climbing, but nothing too long or strenuous.

The Walk

Turn left outside the pub and head north-east along the road for about 200 yards until you come to a small parking area on the right. A path leads from here almost due east, between two rocks. It is not signposted, but is not difficult to find. Soon the path joins a track and begins to descend into the valley. As it does so, look across to the slopes of Birch Tor opposite and you will see four stone enclosures. These are called Ace Fields, and there is a legend attached to them.

It is said that a 17th century Widecombe tin-miner called Jan Reynolds was so desperate for money that he sold his soul to the

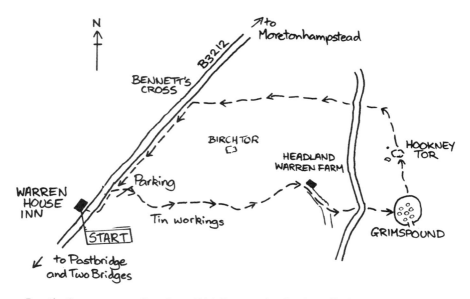

Devil. One stormy Sunday, Old Dewer (as he is called on Dartmoor) came to collect him. He found Jan playing cards during the sermon in Widecombe church, crashed through the roof and whisked him away into the storm on his horse. As they passed over Birch Tor, the aces fell from Jan's pack, and as they hit the ground they turned into these enclosures. It is true that from this angle the one on the far left looks like a diamond and the next along has the approximate shape of a heart. But it takes some imagination to make a club and a spade from the other two.

When the track curves sharply to the left, go straight on down an eroded path, aiming for the path which can clearly be seen going up the other side of the valley. At the bottom of the slope, you cross a a stream, and then a well-worn track. If you fancy making a slight detour, there are the remains of abandoned tin workings all along this valley. Our path, however, leads up the other side, alongside the wall of the fourth of the Ace Fields. Once past the wall, it continues to climb, and then heads downhill towards the farm you can see at the bottom. As it begins to descend, look across to the right and you will see a well-preserved stone row. These stones are thought to have had some special significance in prehistoric times, but exactly what purpose they served – religious, ceremonial or just decorative – is still a matter of conjecture.

At the bottom of the hill, turn right (signposted 'Bridlepath for

Challacombe Farm'). Go down to Headland Warren Farm and cross the farmyard. Just beyond the farm buildings, bear left up to a gate marked 'permitted path'.

Follow the path on the other side up through the bracken to the road. Turn right and follow the road to Firth Bridge. (If you miss the path, do not worry. Just head straight up the hill and you will come to the road.) Firth Bridge is in fact not recognisable as a bridge – it is simply the place where a stream coming down from the opposite hillside goes under the road. Once you have located the stream, however, the path you want is easy to find. It is just to the left of the stream as you look up the hill, up some steps.

Follow the path alongside the stream to the Bronze Age settlement of Grimspound. This is the best-preserved ancient settlement on Dartmoor, and is well worth exploring. The outer wall is believed to have been some 10 ft high originally, and the base is still largely intact. Inside are the remains of a number of stone huts. The whole area powerfully evokes the rigours of life in those far-off days.

Go north from Grimspound (i.e. to the left, along the wall of the settlement), climbing a steep but well-made path up Hookney Tor. It is not signposted, but it is very easy to find. Pause at the top of the tor to catch your breath and admire the magnificent views which open up both in front of you to the north and behind you to the south. Go down the gentler slope on the other side, cross a wall and turn left at the path immediately beyond it. Again there is no signpost, but the path is so well used that you cannot miss it.

This is part of the Two Moors Way, a long-distance route that goes from the southern edge of Dartmoor to the northern edge of Exmoor. After crossing the road it climbs up towards Birch Tor, providing a glorious panoramic view to the right on a clear day, all the way across to North Devon. This path will lead you to the small car park on the B3212 at Bennett's Cross, about ½ mile north-east of the Warren House Inn. Turn left and follow the road back to the pub.

㉕ Princetown
The Plume of Feathers Inn

High, bleak and windy, Princetown's main claim to fame is as the home of Dartmoor Prison, the forbidding grey bulk of which looms over it to the north. The surrounding moorland, however, is magnificent, and the village is a Mecca for walkers.

One major attraction is the High Moorland Visitor Centre, just across the road from the Plume of Feathers. It provides a fascinating exposition of the high moor, including its history, wildlife, people and the activities that take place there today, all in a series of displays, exhibitions and films. There is no entrance charge, and it is well worth a visit if you want to know more about this unique landscape and its background.

Princetown has three pubs and all have their merits, but the Plume of Feathers is my personal choice – and that of most walkers. It is full of atmosphere, with granite walls, slate floors, exposed beams and copper bar tops. There are two bars, both with open fires in winter, a family room and a beer garden, a picnic area and a children's play area at the back. There is also a wide range of accommodation, including an alpine bunkhouse with cooking facilities, and a camping area for 75 tents with a shower and toilet block.

An extensive range of freshly prepared food is available, ranging from sandwiches, paninis and jacket potatoes to main meals, such as steaks and local fish, and coffee and tea are also served throughout the day.

Telephone: 01822 890240.

How to get there: The village is on the B3212 Yelverton to Moretonhampstead road. The Plume of Feathers is on the main road in the centre of the village.

Parking: There is a large car park behind the pub. There should be no problem about leaving your car there while you walk, but do ask first. Alternatively, there is a car park behind the visitors' centre, or you may find parking in the road.

Length of the walk: 5¼ miles. Maps: OS Explorer OL28 Dartmoor; OS Landranger 191 Okehampton and North Dartmoor area (start and finish of the walk), and 202 Torbay and South Dartmoor area (middle section) (GR 591735).

This is a moorland walk par excellence. It gives you a taste of the high moor without too much effort, and you are seldom without a superb view. It is quite undemanding, but you will find stout shoes a help in negotiating some of the rougher ground. Along the way, you will find a feat of 18th century engineering, some interesting old tin workings and the bog that inspired Sir Arthur Conan Doyle's The Hound of the Baskervilles.

The Walk

Take the road which runs alongside the pub to the left, past the garden. Go through the gate at the end on to a track, which leads between walls on to the moor. Look back as you follow this track to get a good view of the grim prison behind you. Go through another gate and keep on the same track, with a wall on your left, South Hessary Tor ahead, Hart Tor to the right and the moors rolling away beyond. Behind you is the television mast on North Hessary Tor, on

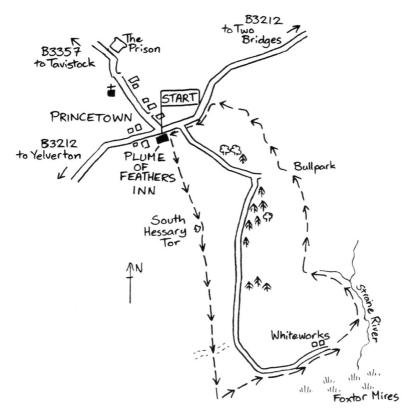

the other side of Princetown, which will act as a kind of beacon for a large part of this walk.

The views to right and left from South Hessary Tor are superb, rolling away in both directions and giving an excellent idea of the vastness of Dartmoor. Beyond South Hessary Tor, keep following the line of the wall. You can see the Devonport Leat shimmering in the distance as it winds away to the left. You will be meeting it again later in the walk.

As the wall turns away to the left, go straight on, still with that lovely view of the moors rolling away on the left. The PCWW (Plymouth City Water Works) marker stones act as excellent route guides.

About a mile from South Hessary Tor, you cross a well-defined track, and another lovely view opens up to the right, this time with Burrator Reservoir and Sheeps Tor in the middle distance, and Cornwall in the distance on a clear day. After another 400 yards, another well-defined track crosses your path. Turn left along it, cross another track and head down to the road which you can see ahead.

Bear right at the road and follow it down to cross the Devonport Leat. This watercourse was built in the 18th century to take water from the West Dart and Cowsic rivers down to Devonport, now part of Plymouth – a distance of 17 miles. Given the need to maintain a constant but gentle downward slope and the tools and techniques available at the time, it was quite a feat, and it has stood the test of time.

Immediately to your right as you follow the road are the old Whiteworks tin workings, and beyond the notorious Foxtor Mires which in the past ensnared many an unwary traveller if the local folklore is to be believed. They formed the inspiration for the Great Grimpen Mire in Sir Arthur Conan Doyle's Sherlock Holmes mystery *The Hound of the Baskervilles* – indeed the whole book had its inspiration in this area, which Conan Doyle visited while staying with friends locally.

The road passes two houses on the left and then goes through some more tin workings. Where it ends go straight on and follow a track to a gate. Go through the gate and bear right initially. Do not cross the stream ahead of you, however, but bear left round the hill, roughly following the course of the stream but a little way above it. There is no clear path here, but the going is fairly easy. As you round the hill, start climbing to join the wall above you, and follow it until it meets another wall.

Turn right and follow the second wall gently down to a footbridge and equally gently up the other side, with South Hessary Tor appearing beyond a plantation on your left, and the mast of North Hessary Tor above Princetown in the distance. At the top of the slope you join a track, still with the wall on your left. A view now opens up ahead of you, dominated by the bulk of Longaford Tor.

At the junction at the end of this field, go left through a gate and into a lane. Just beyond the house on your right, turn right (signposted 'Path'), go through another gate and follow a track which turns to the left and then to the right. At the junction, turn left (signposted 'Public bridlepath to Princetown'). Cross the Devonport Leat again, go through a gate and follow the fence and wall. There are more superb moorland views to the right and behind you.

Soon Princetown appears ahead of you, with the glowering walls of the prison over on the right. Go through another gate on to a track, which winds between a fence and a wall to a road. Turn left and follow the road back to the centre of the village and the pub on your left.

26 Scorriton
The Tradesman's Arms

There is not much to Scorriton – just a few houses, a farm or two, a church and the Tradesman's Arms. The pub was built around 300 years ago to serve the tin-miners from the moor (the 'trade' from which it probably derives its name), and offers a pleasant atmosphere and a friendly welcome. It is frequented by the locals and is also popular with walkers (the Two Moors Way almost passes the door).

There are two bars. The main one has a comfortable sofa in front of an open fire. The snug bar at the back is a cosy inviting little room, but without a fire. Both are very attractively furnished. There is also a beer garden and a family room, a comfortable place with picture windows and extensive views over the surrounding countryside.

A range of bar snacks is available including sandwiches, ploughman's and pasties, as well as daily specials.

Telephone: 01364 631206.

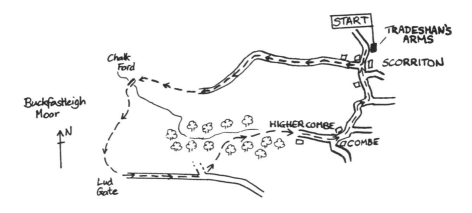

How to get there: The easiest way to approach Scorriton is probably from Buckfast. Leave the A38 Exeter to Plymouth road at Dart Bridge (the Buckfastleigh exit if travelling from the Exeter direction, the Buckfast exit if travelling from Plymouth). Follow the signs to Buckfast, and then follow the road round past Buckfast Abbey and up the hill until you come to a road leading off to the right, signposted to Holne. Follow that road for a little over 2 miles and you will see a sign pointing left to Scorriton. This takes you into the village and the pub is on the right.

The village can also be approached from the Ashburton to Princetown road. Turn off at the Holne signpost, about halfway between Holne Bridge and Newbridge. Follow the signs to Holne and then the signs to Scorriton.

Parking: It is possible, but not always easy, to park in the road. It is best, therefore, to ask the proprietors if you can leave your car in the pub car park. Unless the place is particularly busy, they will generally have no objection.

Length of the walk: 4 miles. Maps: OS Explorer OL28 Dartmoor; OS Landranger 202 Torbay and South Dartmoor area (GR 704685).

There is a bit of everything on this route: moors, woods, farmland and country lanes, with one or two superb views for added interest.

110

The Walk

Turn left outside the pub and then right after a few yards up a long, wide track, which leads you between farm fields up towards the moors. This is part of the Two Moors Way, the long-distance path which runs from the extreme south of Dartmoor all the way to the extreme north of Exmoor. It is a long climb, but you can pause from time to time to catch your breath, and to admire the view which begins to open up behind you, across farms and woods to open moorland.

As you near the top, the track narrows and you pass through a gate. The path then forks and you should take the left-hand route (signposted 'Bridlepath for Chalk Ford and Lud Gate').

Go through a gate and follow this path as it descends, with bracken stretching down to the woods on your left, and to the stream which you can hear but not yet see at the bottom. Go through the gate at the end down to the stream. Cross the footbridge (signposted 'Bridlepath for Lud Gate and Cross Furzes'). At the corner of the fence turn left and follow the fence up the hill. Cross another small stream and follow the line of trees up the slope ahead of you. Although there are fields and trees on your left, you will notice the contrast on your right – open moorland with hardly a tree worthy of the name in sight.

The path soon curves slightly to the right. Pause here for the view across to the left – a patchwork of fields, hedges and woods rolling away to the open moors beyond. Then, as the fence drops away sharply to the left, bear slightly left yourself to join a track down to Lud Gate, which you will see in the fence ahead of you. This gate leads into a narrow track between hedges (signposted 'Public bridlepath Cross Furzes and footpath to Higher Combe').

After about ¼ mile, turn left through a gate into the driveway of Strole (signposted 'Public footpath Higher Combe'). A few yards later turn right through a gate (signposted 'Public footpath'). Turn immediately left to follow the edge of the field, cross a stile and go down the left-hand side of the next field, with views ahead of you across the Dart valley to the moors and tors beyond.

At the bottom of this field, turn right to follow the fence that runs along the bottom, skirting Scae Wood. There are more views of rolling farmland ahead. Go through the gap at the end of the field, turn left and follow the path down to a gate and into Lakemoor Wood.

Within the wood there is a cool, dark track running between high banks. Follow it down until it brings you out at a group of houses and then a lane – this is Higher Combe. Follow the lane to the right until it meets a road, and then turn left. The road curves to the left over a bridge at Combe and up a hill. At the T-junction at the top, turn left again to go into Scorriton. The pub is about 300 yards down the road on the right.

27 Shaldon
The Ness House Hotel

Shaldon is a very pretty village on the Teign estuary, with an attractive centre, a lovely foreshore and tiny lanes climbing up the hillside behind. It is a popular sailing centre, and in summer the view over the water is particularly beautiful with colourful sails shimmering in the sun, and a bustle of activity.

The Ness House Hotel is ideally situated at the top of a headland, known as The Ness, with superb views over the village and the river to Teignmouth. It is an elegant Georgian building, with a very comfortable bar, and a lounge furnished with settees and armchairs. A conservatory area overlooks the river, and there is also a more formal restaurant. The bar serves a wide range of food, from filled baguettes and ploughman's lunches to steaks and a good variety of daily specials. There is a separate restaurant menu.

Telephone 01626 873480

How to get there: Shaldon is on the A379 coast road from Teignmouth to Torquay. At the top of the hill to the west of the village is a turning to a pay and display car park, which is also signposted to the Ness House Hotel.

Parking: There is very little parking at the hotel, so please park in the large pay and display car park opposite it.

Length of the walk: 5 miles. Maps OS Explorer 110 Torquay and Dawlish; OS Landranger 202 Torbay and South Dartmoor area (GR 938720).

The views along this part of the coast are among the most stunning in Devon. Combine them with a lovely stretch of river, two attractive villages and some quiet country lanes, and you have a superb walk of very varied appeal. Such pleasures have to be paid for, however, and in this case the price is some pretty steep climbs, particularly along the coastal path. Note, too, that in wet weather, some of the climbs can become slippery.

The Walk

Turn left as you leave the hotel. Then, as the road bears right, leave it to follow the path that goes straight on, passing the Shaldon Wildlife Trust on the left.

You might like to visit the Trust, an attractive little zoo containing small mammals, exotic birds and some invertebrates. Most of the animals are zoo bred, and the Trust is a breeding centre for endangered species. It is open throughout the year.

The path climbs gently between banks. As you climb, look out for some steps on the left, with a yellow waymark on a post. Climb the steps and you will find yourself high above the red sands of Ness Beach. The red is typical of this stretch of coast, and you will be passing red cliffs and beaches all the way along.

Keep to the left of the small golf course, go through a gap in the hedge and keep to the left again. At the end of the golf course cross a stile and go down some steps to a field. There is a steep but fairly short climb up the other side of the field, and at the top you can look back along the coast for a breathtaking view of Teignmouth and the red cliffs towards Dawlish, and then the whiter cliffs beyond the Exe estuary and all the way round to Portland Bill in Dorset.

Go through the gap in the fence into the next field, still keeping to the left. At the top, the view ahead opens up, around Babbacombe Bay. Not quite as spectacular as the one behind you, it is nevertheless an attractive outlook, with the red of the cliffs contrasting with the green of the fields above.

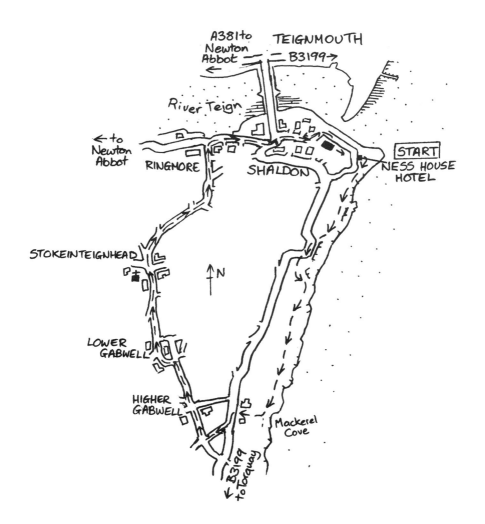

At the end of this field, cross the stile on the right to the road. Turn left past a house to find a path leading between a fence and a bank which protects you from the traffic (signposted 'Coast Path'). At the end, go up some steps to join the road. It is a very busy road, but there is a pavement along this stretch as the road curves to the right. After the bend, where the pavement ends, turn left down some steps (signposted 'Coast Path'). The path descends fairly steeply between two fences, and then levels off as it passes a modern house on the left.

It turns right to follow the coast for about 100 yards, and then turns right again for a steep climb inland. Pause at the top to catch your breath and enjoy another look back along this stunning coastline. The path curves to the left and you come to a junction. Go straight on and the view across Babbacome Bay opens up ahead of you again.

The climbing resumes as you go steeply down and enter a little copse. This is followed by another steep ascent, with steps to make the going easier, and another steep descent down the other side. The next climb is rather gentler, with views both ways along the coast at the top. You go down yet again, and then mercifully have a fairly long level stretch, followed by a comparatively gentle climb. You cross various stiles as you go.

At the junction at the top, go right (signposted to Higher Gabwell). The path runs between a fence on the left and a hedge on the right up to a track. Turn left and follow the track to the road, where you turn left again. After about 50 yards turn right down Longpark Hill. The gently rolling hills you can see to your right are a far cry from the rugged coastline you have just left behind, but provide an appealing backdrop for all that.

At the crossroads, turn right and follow the lane as it winds peacefully through Gabwell to Stokeinteignhead. There is quite a lot of modern (and generally uninspiring) housing en route, but the centre of the village is very pretty.

A few yards beyond the post office, turn right up Forches Hill and climb steadily out of the village. At the top there is another superb view: up the valley of the Teign and over the hills to Dartmoor on the left, and across to Teignmouth and round the coast to Portland Bill.

Follow the lane down the hill and at the fork bear left to descend steeply to a T-junction. Turn right and follow the road down and alongside the river, with a great deal of birdlife on the mudflats at low tide. All too soon, you leave the river and join the main road for a few hundred yards. As the road turns left to cross Shaldon Bridge, go straight on into the village centre. It is a delightful place, with cottages and shops clustered around the square and up the hillside. Pass through and follow the road alongside the water and then up to the right. The hotel is on your left.

28 **South Brent**
The Royal Oak

The Royal Oak is a pleasant, unpretentious pub in a pleasant, unpretentious village. It is almost 200 years old, and the local court was once held there; the old judge's chair is still a feature of the bar.

There is just the one, L-shaped bar, with an open fire in one arm of the L. It is well furnished and carpeted, and it is refreshing to find that no attempt has been made to 'prettify' it with mock-traditional beams and horse brasses. It looks just what it is – a good early 19th century inn, very much a local, but offering a warm welcome to visitors. An interesting feature is that they offer the chance to do some ceramic painting, so that you can take away a souvenir or gift!

A good range of food is on offer, and there is a Sunday roast lunch (for which booking is advised). Dishes range from light meals such as ploughman's lunches, sandwiches and pasties to more substantial specials.

Telephone: 01364 72133.

How to get there: South Brent is just north of the A38 Exeter to Plymouth road, and is clearly signposted from it. The Royal Oak is in Station Road, in the centre of the village.

Parking: The pub has no parking, but there is a free public car park at the old station, about 50 yards up the road. Parking is also possible in the road, but it is restricted to one hour at a time from Monday to Saturday.

Length of the walk: 4¼ miles. Maps: OS Explorer OL28 Dartmoor; OS Landranger 202 Torbay and South Dartmoor area (GR 698602).

This beautiful, undemanding and varied walk follows the valley of the river Avon upstream to Shipley Bridge and then back down the other side. It includes a delightful amble alongside the river itself, but also some quiet and attractive lanes and a couple of stretches of pleasant woodland. There are also some good views up, down and across the valley from time to time.

The Walk

Turn left outside the pub and follow Station Road for about 50 yards to the car park at the old station. Turn left and go through the car park. On the other side turn left again and almost immediately sharp right on to a track just before the church (signposted 'Public footpath Lydia Bridge'). The track leads down and under a railway bridge to a kissing-gate.

Beyond the gate, the path curves to the left to run alongside the river Avon. This is an idyllic spot, with the sunshine filtering through the trees and the river sparkling and tumbling over the boulders on your left. It is particularly lovely in spring, when the rhododendrons which line the right-hand side of the path are a mass of colour, and in autumn, with the rich golds and browns of the turning leaves.

Towards the end of this stretch, there are some most attractive houses on the opposite bank of the river. A series of steps lead up to a stone stile into a lane. Turn left to cross Lydia Bridge and follow the lane round a right-hand bend. A few yards beyond the bend, look out for a path leading off to the right between two walls. There is a public footpath sign, but it is not visible from the lane – it is a few yards up the path by a stile, and points to Avon Cott.

Cross the stile and follow a narrow path between two walls. You can still hear the river over on the right, and soon the walls end and you find yourself walking between a bank on the left and a lovely wood stretching down the steep slope on the right. Cross the stone stile at the end into a field and go straight across to a stone stile on the other side. Do *not* go to the wooden stile in the far right-hand corner.

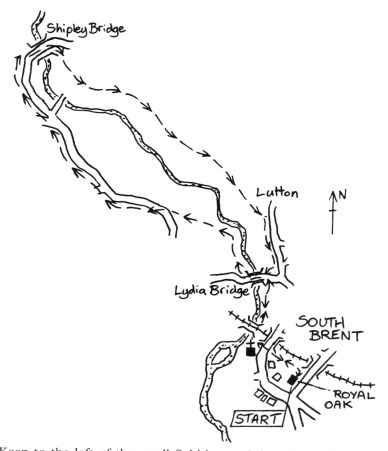

Keep to the left of the small field beyond the stile, and you come to another stone stile. Cross it and then cross the bracken-covered 'slope on the other side. This ends in another stile, which leads into another field, with very good views ahead, behind and to the right. Cross to the far corner of this field and go over a stone stile into a lane. Turn right.

Our route follows this lane for a total of abut 1 ½ miles. It is pleasant walking, with the occasional view through the trees and the river down to the right. At the road junction, ignore the turning to the left and go straight on. The lane winds down to join the river, follows it upstream for about 250 yards and then climbs away to the left. Ignore the roads leading off to the left and right and carry straight on (signposted to Shipley Bridge).

About 500 yards further on, the lane curves to the right and Shipley Tor comes into view ahead. Soon you cross a cattle grid and come to the Shipley Bridge car park. There are toilets here if you need them. Follow the lane round to the right, cross Shipley Bridge and follow it round to the right again. Just after the cattle grid, turn right through a gate. For some reason the signpost, which points to Lutton via Didworthy for South Brent, is some three yards beyond the gate, but it is quite clear where you have to go.

After a few yards you cross a stile and bear left to skirt the top of a wood. Go through a gateway and along a broad path, with a wall on your left and the woods stretching down to the river on the right. Cross a stile, and then, after about 100 yards, another one. The path goes between two banks and then opens up, providing a lovely view across the valley to the right.

The path then goes downhill and crosses a farmyard to a gate and a lane. Cross the lane to a drive on the other side (signposted 'Public bridlepath Lutton'). At the entrance to Pinewood Lodge at the end of the drive, take the path which branches off to the left, with a bank on the right and a fence on the left. This leads into some trees and to a gate. Beyond the gate, you have a bracken-covered slope on the left and a wall on the right, with Overbrent Wood on the other side.

Go through another gate and follow the path between low walls, with a steep slope down to the river on your right. Go through yet another gate, to be met with superb views down, up and across the Avon valley. The path now broadens into a track and leads gently down to another gate. It then winds steeply down, through one more gate, to a ford.

Cross the stream via a stone slab to the right of the ford and follow the track up to the left. Turn right at the lane at the end and then left after a few yards as the main lane goes right. Go through the gate at the end (signposted 'Public footpath') and keep to the left of the field on the other side. There are beautiful moorland views to the right and behind you.

Cross the stile at the end of the field and then cut across to a gate in the wall on the left-hand side of the next field, and into a lane. Turn right and follow the lane down a steep hill. Turn right at the T-junction, and just before the bridge turn left across a stone stile (signposted 'Public footpath South Brent'). This takes you back along the riverbank. At the end turn sharp left, go through the car park and turn right at the end to return to the pub.

Torcross
The Start Bay Inn

Torcross is popular with visitors, mainly because it is at one end of the superb Slapton Sands, 3 miles of continuous beach stretching all the way to Pilchard Cove, just below Strete. Its other attraction is its proximity to Slapton Ley, a beautiful freshwater lake and nature reserve, and the subject of this walk.

The Ley is separated from the beach by a ridge, formed by a rise in sea level at the end of the last ice age which pushed shingle up the shore. This ridge has prevented river water from escaping to the sea and so formed the large freshwater lake you see today.

The Start Bay Inn is ideally placed for both attractions. It faces the promenade alongside the beach, with benches and tables outside on the pavement for customers to sit and enjoy the view, and at the back it overlooks the Ley. It is an attractive thatched building dating back to the 14th century, an old coaching inn on the main route from Dartmouth to Kingsbridge. It is pleasant inside, with low beams and little alcoves, and a family room at one end.

A full range of food is available from bar snacks to main meals. The pub is renowned for its seafood, which is guaranteed to be fresh because it is caught by the landlord himself! The range is impressive: from cod and haddock to monkfish and skate.

Telephone: 01548 580553.

How to get there: Torcross is on the A379 Dartmouth to Kingsbridge road, at the Kingsbridge end of Slapton Sands. The Start Bay Inn is right on this road.

Parking: The pub has its own car park, and there will usually be no objection to customers leaving their cars while they walk in winter. However, do ask before doing so. It becomes very busy during the summer so, at that time, please park in the large pay and display car park almost opposite the pub.

Length of the walk: 4½ miles. Maps: OS Explorer OL20 South Devon; OS Landranger 202 Torbay and South Dartmoor area (GR 823422).

This delightful and easy walk has a great deal to interest naturalists, especially bird-watchers, but should also appeal to anyone with an eye for the natural beauty of Slapton Ley and its diverse habitats.

The Walk

Cross the main road behind the pub and turn to the right to the public car park a few yards down the road. At the start of the car park, you will find an old Second World War tank which was dredged from the sea, and which now stands as a memorial to the 1,000 American soldiers who were killed in 1944 during an exercise in preparation for the Normandy landings.

Cross the car park to the public bird hide for a closer view of this end of Slapton Ley and the birdlife to be found there. Coots, moorhens and swans are common, but the Ley is also an important resting and feeding place for migrating birds, and a large number also over-winter here. It is a site of some importance, both nationally and internationally, and the best times for bird-watchers are spring and autumn, when the greatest variety of species is likely to be seen.

After visiting the hide, go through the gap at the end of the car park

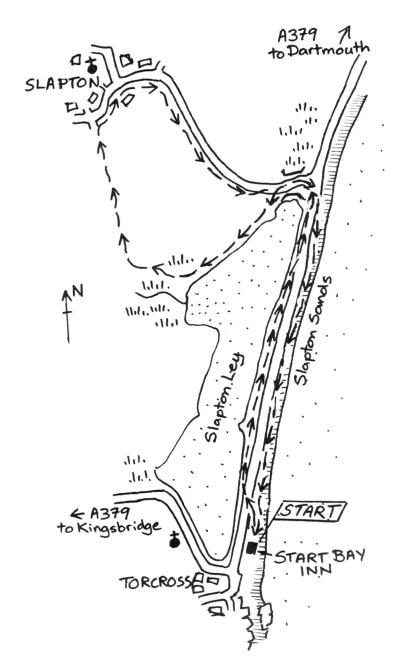

A379
to Dartmouth

SLAPTON

↑N

Slapton Ley

Slapton Sands

← A379
to Kingsbridge

START

START BAY
INN

TORCROSS

furthest from the pub, on to a path which runs alongside the Ley, between it and the road. There are further opportunities to see the birds as you wander along this path, but probably not as clearly as from the hide, as the water is edged with reeds. You may be vaguely aware of the noise from the road on your right, but it is not intrusive, and this is a delightful stroll, with wild flowers all alongside the path, the Ley on the left and the rich, red earth of the fields stretching up beyond.

The path is easy, and runs in a more or less straight line for about 1 ½ miles. It ends at the road from the A379 into Slapton village. Turn left here, cross Slapton Bridge and turn left again (signposted 'Public footpath Deer Lane'). This path takes you past a boathouse and along the very edge of the Ley. It is a delightful route, with the water lapping the shore on your left and trees and wild flowers on your right. There are usually several students by the water's edge or in boats, studying the abundant insect, animal, bird and plant life.

Follow the edge of the Ley, crossing two stiles. There are a few brief climbs up the bank where the shore is impassable, but nothing at all strenuous. After a while you pass over a short boardwalk and into some trees, only to emerge soon afterwards into a glade. Go straight across. The path curves to the right, away from the Ley, into Southgrounds Coppice, which is full of spring and summer flowers.

At the gate, turn left (signposted 'Permissive route Slapton village') to follow a meandering boardwalk across a marsh, with reeds closing in on either side. This marsh is an important habitat for a variety of species, including warblers, otters and plants like willowherb and orchids.

Ignore the first turning to the right, along another boardwalk, but take the next, after a few yards (signposted 'Public footpath Slapton village'). The path takes you past a wastewater treatment works to a track. Follow it straight up, past a nursery, to join a lane. Turn right and follow the lane into Slapton, a charming old village of traditional thatched and stone cottages with an attractive church.

Go up the hill to a T-junction and turn right. As you leave the village, you will find the Slapton Ley Field Centre on your left. Here you can obtain more information on the reserve. About 600 yards down the road from the field centre is Slapton Bridge. After crossing the bridge you can either turn right to return to Torcross the way you came or, if you would like a bit of variety, you can cross the A379 to Slapton Sands and go back along the beach, paddling in the dead calm sea or collecting some of the pretty shells and pebbles.

Merrivale
The Dartmoor Inn

Merrivale is little more than a dot on the map. It comprises a few farms and houses and the Dartmoor Inn, and not much else. Until recently it was the site of a large granite quarry – the last outpost of a once thriving Dartmoor industry. This has now gone the way of the other sites, having closed at the end of the last century, but the workings still form a backdrop to the Dartmoor Inn, which lies in the valley below.

The pub was originally a row of 17th century cottages. It has a long lounge bar with a large granite fireplace at one end, and a smaller public bar leading off it. The lounge is decorated with chinaware; there are plates along the walls and jugs, mugs teapots and chamber pots hanging from the beams. Outside there are tables and benches, from which you get a lovely view over the river Walkham and Dartmoor. The menu ranges from ploughman's lunches, salads and soups to a good selection of main courses.

Telephone: 01822 890340.

How to get there: Merrivale is on the B3357 between Tavistock and Princetown, and the Dartmoor Inn is just off the road.

Parking: There is limited parking in the side road just beyond the pub, but there is also a car park at the top of the hill to the east, and you could start the walk from there.

Length of the walk: 5 miles. Maps: OS Explorer OL28 Dartmoor; OS Landranger 191 Okehampton and North Dartmoor area (GR 549742).

This route takes you up to the most extensive collection of ancient remains on Dartmoor and then across the moor to some of the old granite quarries that were a feature of this part of Dartmoor. The homeward leg follows pretty country lanes and farm tracks. There is a steep climb from the pub to the moor, and another, less arduous one further on, but the views from the open moor are worth the effort.

The Walk

Turn left from the pub and follow the road up the hill to the east. Just beyond the car park at the top, bear right along a well-worn path, aiming in the general direction of the mast on North Hessary Tor, which is clearly visible above the horizon. As the path becomes less clear, aim slightly to the right of the mast. You will notice the remains of a cluster of Bronze Age huts on the left as you go, and as you come over the hill a stone row will become visible ahead of you. On the other side is a leat, and there is a second stone row beyond that.

No one is quite sure what purpose these rows (of which there are over 70 on Dartmoor) served. It appears that they had some ritual significance, probably to do with burial, since most are associated with burial sites. But exactly why they were erected is unclear. Turn right at the second row and follow it. On your left you will see a kistvaen, an ancient burial chamber which would originally have had a cairn over it, and just beyond it a burial mound in the centre of the row itself. Turn left here and cross to a stone circle and a standing stone by a wall. As with the stone rows, no one is sure exactly what purpose these structures served, but it was almost certainly something to do with rituals. When you reach the wall, turn left and follow it. When it turns right, follow it round and cross a stream (you may have to go a little way upstream to find a crossing place). Make your way up the hill ahead towards King's Tor.

Just before you reach the tor you will come to a track; this is part of the now dismantled Plymouth and Dartmoor Railway, which was built

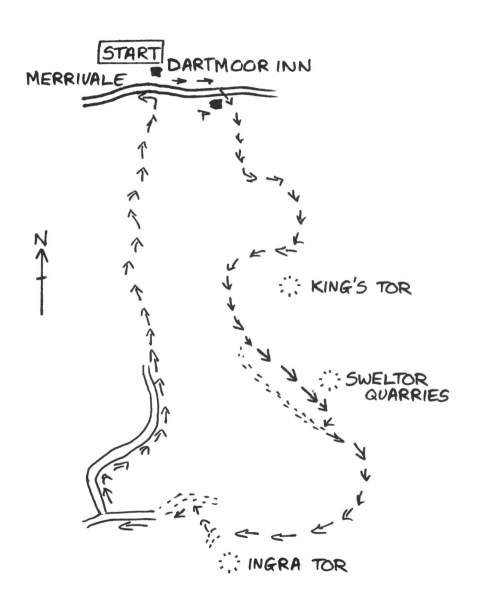

START
MERRIVALE   DARTMOOR INN

N

KING'S TOR

SWELTOR
QUARRIES

INGRA TOR

to transport granite from the area to Plymouth for shipment. Turn right, and as you do so look right for a very good view over the northern part of Dartmoor. As the track curves to the left, you get another magnificent view ahead of you. When the track forks, go left towards Swelltor Quarries. As you follow this track, you will see several carved pieces of granite alongside it. These are corbels that were quarried and carved for the widening of London Bridge in 1903 but were not needed and were therefore left by the side of the railway.

Soon you will come to the quarry itself; follow the track through it and when it ends turn right and make your way down to another track, which is a continuation of the main dismantled railway, which you left at the fork. Turn left and follow it as it swings right. Go over one bridge and under another. Cross a narrow wooden bridge and just beyond it, as the track swings left round Ingra Tor, turn right off it and go down towards the valley, following a broad grassy path. It takes you to a roughly surfaced track; turn left and follow it to a lane. Continue along the lane to a crossroads.

Turn right (signposted to Daveytown) and follow the lane down between hedges to cross a river. When it ends, go straight on up a track (signposted to Merrivale), through four gates. The track climbs through some trees to another gate. It winds among rocks and crosses a river. It then goes through two gates into a farmyard. Cross the farmyard to a surfaced track, and follow that with the river Walkham on your left. Go through another gate into another farmyard and across to the B3357 and turn left to cross the river and return to the pub.